The Feeling Intellect

The Feeling Intellect

Reading the Bible with C. S. Lewis

ROGER J. NEWELL

WIPF & STOCK · Eugene, Oregon

THE FEELING INTELLECT
Reading the Bible with C. S. Lewis

Copyright © 2010 Roger J. Newell. All rights reserved. Except for brief quotations
in critical publications or reviews, no part of this book may be reproduced in any
manner without prior written permission from the publisher. Write: Permissions,
Wipf and Stock Publishers, 199 W. 8th Ave., Suite 3, Eugene, OR 97401.

Wipf & Stock
An Imprint of Wipf and Stock Publishers
199 W. 8th Ave., Suite 3
Eugene, OR 97401
www.wipfandstock.com

ISBN 13: 978-1-60899-138-9

Manufactured in the U.S.A.

The Scripture quotations in this publication are from the Revised Standard Version
of the Bible, copyrighted 1946, 1952, 1971, and 1973 by the Division of Christian
Education of the National Council of the Churches of Christ in the U.S.A., and used
by permission.

To the Mota Bota Fellowship. With thanksgiving.

Contents

Preface ix

PART ONE: AN EXPERIMENT IN READING SCRIPTURE

Introduction: The Experiment · 3

1   Response and Responsibility (Luke 1–2) · 9

2   Atonement: Aslan's How (Rom 3–5) · 25

3   Freedom for a Horse, His Boy, and Western Culture
    (Or Nurturing Narnians in a Calormen Culture) (Gal 4) · 39

4   Till We Have Christians: A Myth of Christendom Retold (Matt 20) · 49

PART TWO: READING THE BIBLE AS A DOUBLE NARRATIVE

5   A Theology of Nature and of Grace
    for a Silent Planet (Ps 19; Rom 1–2) · 63

6   Of Inner Rings and Rivals: Rehabilitating
    the Doctrine of Election (Gen 27; Rom 9–11) · 74

7   "Gawd, Ain't It Lovely?"
    The Journey from Fear to Awe (Prov 1; Acts 4) · 83

8   Curses for Babylonians and Crumbs for Canaanites: A Hermeneutical
    Regress for Contemporary Pilgrims (Ps 137; Gen 22; Deut 7; Matt 15) · 91

Bibliography 107
Scripture Index 111
Subject/Name Index 113

Preface

CHRISTIANS OF ALL SORTS agree that the Bible is the unique source-book for our understanding and knowledge of God. Yet reading the Bible is often as neglected in believers' homes as amongst the skeptics. Moreover, there is much evidence that the Bible is as often misread in the modern church as we suppose it to have been widely misunderstood in the darkest days of medieval superstition. Misinterpretations seem further fueled by the endless outpourings from experts of various pedigrees filling bookstalls with articles and books claiming to have uncovered the real meaning of a text misunderstood for centuries by the Church until its real meaning was uncovered by our intrepid modern scholar. Faced with this combination of media publicity, cultural ignorance, and personal searching, it would be an enormous help to sit with a deeply learned scholar, devoted to the historic Christian faith, and yet who taught with the common touch, to help us mature in our reading of Scripture. Such tutorials might rekindle our desire to read the Bible more skillfully with the humble discipline of daily practice.

C. S. Lewis has inspired a generation of readers, both skilled and beginners, to deepen their understanding and enjoyment of Scripture. As a teacher of many kinds of ancient literature, he brought out the best in his students as readers at the same time that he brought out deep insight into the meaning of texts. This double movement of bringing the best out of the reader and the best out of the text is what I hope to contribute to in these chapters. My goal is, through conversation with Lewis, to read Scripture with a scholar's trained attention as well as a disciple's desire to follow the truth of the gospel wherever it leads. My strategy along the way will include asking questions such as these: How can we read this ancient library of books in the way it deserves to be read? How can we avoid paying it unhelpful compliments that distort its meaning? How can we truly hear a message so beyond us in its beauty, goodness, and truth that it makes us feel undone and we are tempted to say with Peter, "Depart from me, Lord, for I am a wicked man" (Luke 5:8)? How can we bring our most creative, careful, and honest selves to the reading of Scripture without becoming discouraged or sidetracked along the way?

Over many years of lively conversations with students, colleagues, and friends, many have told me there were times, sometimes for long stretches, when Lewis was the significant mentor of their faith journey. Something about the personal warmth of his style combined with the relentless honesty, the wit, the penetrating, "feeling intellect" made him an essential companion. For many of us, Lewis has been the Mr. Greatheart who wouldn't let us quit, the Faithful Friend who accompanied us in encounters with Giants of Despair, Castles of Doubt, and countless Vanity Fairs. Consistently he helped us face the dangers unsentimentally, inspiring us to see beyond the glitter, projections, and half truths that con us into supposing the broad path is really the narrow way.

This sense of accompaniment has been the reason for my desire to read the Bible with C. S. Lewis and to read it using the "method" I have learned from him. I invite readers to join with me in this conversation in the spirit that Lewis describes in his chapter on friendship in *The Four Loves*. Such a gathering is the opposite of an inner ring; it includes a deep sense of gratitude for the company that has surrounded us thus far, including a great cloud of witnesses. But it also is an open communion, anticipating that as the conversation continues, the company (the sharing of bread) will continue to widen as well as deepen. Such a way of gathering also inspires hope for when the way seems impossibly difficult. Many times in reading Scripture, despite all my training in the church and the academy, I have gotten stuck as meaning dried up. Then I have turned to one of his essays, a "Narnicle," or an erudite tomb of literary criticism, and I would find myself nudged along, mind and heart somehow opened again to believe and to desire to practice the faith rather than be content merely to read about it.

These chapters have come out of my ongoing conversations with Scripture and Lewis, "using" the way of the feeling intellect he has modeled to help me listen more attentively, to help me pay attention to what I've almost trained myself to ignore, sometimes to loan me the faith to ask awkward questions that orient my heart and mind once again in their homeward direction. In any conversation, there are times for listening as well as times for speaking. My agenda is not to detail or define Lewis's view of Scripture. That has already been sufficiently explored.[1] Nor do I seek to systematically expound what Lewis says *about* the various doctrines of Christianity.[2] Instead my goal has been to explore certain classic texts in conversation with Lewis's writings, asking him questions, looking for insights into meaning, and inviting others into the conversation about issues that Lewis may not have addressed. Should my own voice threaten to dominate the conversation, I hope the other two dialogue partners, Lewis and Scripture, will minimize the confusion and get us back to the task of reading Scripture with the purpose the Church has always had in mind.

I first encountered Lewis when I was sixteen years old and looking for reasons to stay in the church as my peers were rapidly exiting toward the greener pastures of secular life. From the day I began to read *The Screwtape Letters,* I sensed there was much more to Christianity than I had begun to imagine. As time went by, along with the reading of many more Lewis books, the opportunity came to do a doctoral dissertation on Lewis. Over the years of being a pastor and a college teacher that have followed, I have read (and quoted) from most, if not all, of Lewis's writings, including his literary criticism, children's stories, poetry, sermons, and commentaries. I have also inevitably broadened my reading of theology. That larger conversation is part of the mix in these chapters.

In this book I have been drawn toward certain themes and texts in order to abide more deeply in their meaning. They are a selection from an ongoing conversation, chosen because they have gripped my attention or puzzled me and so I have sought to listen with skills and habits tutored by years of reading Lewis. Of course, the conclusions or perspectives I come to in this "trialogue" in no way have his *imprimatur.* I am not seeking to establish an inner ring of Lewisianity. Other readers of Lewis will quite rightly have different views and descriptions of how Lewis has guided their reading of Scripture. My hope for the reader is that by joining with me in this conversation, we shall all gain further maturity reading the Bible because we have spent time reading the Bible with our imaginations baptized, thanks in no small part to conversations with C. S. Lewis. I also hope that these experiments bring together interpretation *and* enjoyment, academic *and* contemplative reading, and will bear fruit in grateful witness.

1. Cf. Christensen, *C. S. Lewis on Scripture.*
2. Cf. Vaus, *Mere Theology, A Guide to the Thought of C. S. Lewis.*

PART ONE

An Experiment in Reading Scripture

Introduction

The Experiment

INDWELLING THE TEXT

H AVE YOU EVER READ a book in such a way that you not only took in the main ideas, themes, and plot but something further also happened? It's as though the text gave you entrance into *the emotion embedded within the story.* C. S. Lewis tells his friend Arthur Greeves that he will never read *Beowulf* correctly unless he is willing to "forget your previous ideas of what a book should be and try and put yourself back in the position of the people for whom it was first made. When I was reading it, I tried to imagine myself as an old Saxon thane sitting in my hall of a winter's night, with the wolves and storm outside and the old fellow singing his story. In this way, you get the atmosphere of terror that runs through it . . ."[1]

In other words, we can open our minds in both a cognitive and affectional way to what is *embedded* in the text. The *feeling intellect* is a phrase used by Lewis (and by Charles Williams and earlier by William Wordsworth) to describe a way of reading in which both reason and imagination are equally alert and at their fullest capacity of insight and creativity.[2] This way of reading never imposes a pre-arranged doctrine or order onto the text to reinforce a traditional explanation. Nor does it transplant the text into an emotional mood acquired elsewhere. Instead,

---

1. Hooper, *They Stand Together,* 143. Elsewhere Lewis writes: "You must, so far as in you lies, become an Achaean chief while reading Homer, a medieval knight while reading Malory, and an eighteenth century Londoner while reading Johnson. Only thus will you be able to judge the work 'in the same spirit that its author writ' and to avoid chimerical criticism." *A Preface to Paradise Lost,* 64.

2. "Williams and the Arthuriad," 285.

the reader receptively *indwells* the text—that is, allows the intrinsic meaning to form its own imprint.

But can one really distinguish embedded ideas and feelings from those that originate elsewhere? Consider, says Lewis, two Englishman on a tour of the continent. The one carries his Englishness abroad with him and brings it home unchanged. He consorts with English tourists along the way. "By a good hotel, he means one that's like an English hotel . . . He complains of bad tea when he might have had excellent coffee . . . But there is another sort of traveling and another sort of reading." One may eat local food, drink local wines, and see a foreign country as it looks to the inhabitants, not the tourists. "You can come home modified, thinking and feeling as you did not think and feel before."[3]

This analogy invites us to choose one of two ways to read a book. We may read to find evidence of theories or ideas that we already value and hunt for hints of them in a hidden or primitive state. Alternatively, we may read in a less calculating way—not to confirm previous opinions or experiences but to encounter new realities, perhaps not yet part of our world. Because this latter way pays careful attention to what is *within* the text, we allow ourselves to be altered by the text we are reading. This launching into a new reality can be described as a baptism, at least while we are in the act of reading. Though a permanent alteration is hardly established, something fresh has been planted within us from the text. At least while we read, we are being changed.

The first time Lewis mentions having his imagination baptized comes, not when reading Scripture, but while reading George MacDonald's novel, *Phantastes*.[4] Believing God had come personally to space, time, and history in and through Jesus, Mary's son, MacDonald invited Lewis to see the entire world *through* this implicit lens. Only later did Lewis choose to live his entire life baptized into the story of Christ. But MacDonald set Lewis's mind on a new path, baptizing his imagination with a christocentric vision of all earth and sky, parents, children, friends, and lovers.

Lewis understood even this temporary baptism to be a process of death and rebirth. In a memorable description, he sees this process as the crux of what he calls good reading.

---

3. Lewis, *Studies in Medieval and Renaissance Literature*, 3.
4. Lewis, *Surprised by Joy*, 171.

Good reading, therefore, though it is not essentially an affectional or moral or intellectual activity, has something in common with all three. In love we escape from our self into one other. In the moral sphere, every act of justice or charity involves putting ourselves in the other person's place and thus transcending our own competitive particularity. In coming to understand anything we are rejecting the facts as they are for us in favour of the facts as they are. The primary impulse of each is to maintain and aggrandize himself. The secondary impulse is to go out of the self, to correct its provincialism and heal its loneliness. In love, in virtue, in the pursuit of knowledge, and in the reception of the arts, we are doing this. Obviously this process can be described either as an enlargement or as a temporary annihilation of the self. But that is an old paradox; 'he that loseth his life shall save it'.[5]

THE EXPERIMENT

My proposal in this book is to make explicit what is implicit in Lewis's reading strategy and apply it to reading Scripture. Specifically, I will follow Lewis's way of responding to the text in three ways: *First, to historically and imaginatively reconstruct (or at least seek to be aware of) the original context. Second, to indwell the emotional as well as the cognitive content embedded in the text, which will lead, third, to a fresh response of discipleship in our contemporary setting.*

Before we look at our first passage, I want to describe this threefold process a little further. If the goal of reading is to be *cognitively and emotionally* immersed in the text, one can't bypass a careful scholarly reconstruction of the cultural and historical context. It's no good trying to imagine ourselves as Saxon thanes while reading Beowulf if we have no clue about the culture, history, and language out of which this ancient tale arises. In Lewis's own literary critical writings, he spent a good deal of energy seeking to recover as accurately as possible the historical context in order to read the text "in the same spirit as the author writ."[6] His introduction to medieval literature, *The Discarded Image*, is a good example of a book-length attempt to provide "an outfit" or map to help contemporary readers enter a worldview everywhere assumed in medieval culture but that has become quite foreign to us. He assembles this outfit in order that

5. Lewis, *An Experiment in Criticism*, 138.

6. Lewis, *A Preface to Paradise Lost*, 64.

readers may enter as fully as possible into the world and characters of medieval stories. In this way Lewis rejects the strategy of "the many" who prefer to *use* ancient literature to see what sort of impression it makes on an unrepentant contemporary mindset. His goal is the very opposite: to read the ancient writings as far as possible from within the worldview inhabited by the ancients. Only thus may a modern reader hope to grasp what these stories meant to those who first told, heard, and recorded them. The better our appreciation of medieval history, philosophy, language, geography, and religion, the better our chance of a cognitive and emotional grasp of the meaning. This logic applies for reading any piece of ancient literature, including the Bible.

Of course, even after we attempt this kind of intellectually rigorous and imaginatively sensitive reading, we still must decide what kind of truth the text possesses. But without grasping the meaning of a text through the disciplined use of both the imagination and the intellect, the question of truth is premature. After all, a meaningless statement or event can be neither true nor false.[7]

This emphasis on the use of imagination as the means to recover meaning may remind some readers of the *Lectio Divina*, the tradition of contemplative reading lived out in monastic communities, or even more specifically the *Ignatian* method, whereby one takes a Bible story and seeks to get inside it by imaginatively identifying with one or more characters as the drama unfolds. By reading the text as if we were that person, we "hear" what God wants to say to us today through this character.[8] Perhaps, on the other hand, insisting on the use of the intellect to accurately grasp the historical-cultural context may remind us of early Protestants like Martin Luther or John Calvin who stressed the historical context as the key to the meaning of Scripture. These Reformers were seeking to recover the historical, *literal* meaning of the text, which they believed had become entangled in allegorical and devotional embellishments that, like weeds, had grown around the text, choking off its intended meaning.[9]

---

7. Lewis, "Bluspels and Flalansferes, A Semantic Nightmare," 157. "But it must not be supposed that I am in any sense putting forward the imagination as the organ of truth. We are not talking of truth, but of meaning: meaning which is the antecedent condition both of truth and falsehood, whose antithesis is not error but nonsense."

8. Casey, *Sacred Reading, The Ancient Art of Lectio Divina*, 52.

9. For further discussion see Thiselton, *New Horizons in Hermeneutics*, 184.

Lewis's wisdom is to incorporate the strengths of both approaches while carefully controlling their limitations. Unlike the imaginatively florid allegorical method, much admired from Origen and Augustine through the medieval period, Lewis reigns in an undisciplined imagination that refuses to do rigorous historical/cultural homework, lest it make the text a nose of wax for popular fads or the latest *Zeitgeist.* Unlike the Ignatian strategy (which clearly has similarity with what Lewis attempts), this way insists that before we try to "hear" what God is saying *to us* in the story, we must first and firmly set ourselves aside and listen to what the story meant to its primary agents and recipients, including both its cognitive content *and* emotional impact. As for the particular temptations of *devotional* reading, I will wait until we consider our first text. Regarding the Luther/Calvin strategy, I suspect Lewis would say that a recovery of the literal, historical context, while essential, only does half the reading job. *A faithful recovery of the historical, literal meaning will also quite properly entail a recovery of the feeling tone or emotional response embedded in the narrative.*

That leaves the third and final task for any contemporary reader, that is, for those of us who are committed to responding with the modesty and honor that comes from confessing to be disciples. It is to ask the Spirit who inspired the text to bring the ancient meaning to bear on our present situation. By referring to modesty, I remind myself that, for example, when reading the opening chapters of Luke, I am neither Jesus nor Mary nor Joseph. By the mention of honor I hope to measure with proper weight the invitation the text makes to include all contemporary readers, "you in your small corner and I in mine" as recipients of good news.

In fact, we live two thousand years further along. The Roman Empire is ancient history. Not too long ago, Francis Fukuyama rather triumphantly suggested we live at the *end of history.* In the wake of the events of 9/11, others have described our epoch as the beginning of the end of the post-cold war *American empire.* Whichever verdict is more accurate, the events and writings of the New Testament have a unique relevance to contemporary readers such that our responses are neither disregarded nor irrelevant to the ongoing, corporate response of Jesus's disciples to this ancient narrative. The more faithfully we indwell the meaning of the text, aware of its context and effect as experienced by the original characters and earliest circle of readers, the more faithful shall we respond within our contemporary situation, personally *and* socio-politically.

In what follows, I will use the experiment provoked by Lewis, sometimes in conversation with his own textual commentary, sometimes extending the discussion to include further questions raised by this approach, as well as in conversation with contemporary events. To attempt this in any exhaustive survey of the entire Bible is beyond my scope. But I hope that the texts I engage in this manner will encourage the reader's fresh baptism into their meaning. At least while reading these texts, I hope to be nearby, holding the font. My goal is to show how a receptive, obedient imagination yoked with responsible historical reconstruction will encourage a discipleship that honors both the glory and affliction of divine initiative and human response.

1

Response and Responsibility (Luke 1–2)

In the sixth month the angel Gabriel was sent by God to a town in Galilee called Nazareth, to a virgin engaged to a man whose name was Joseph, of the house of David. The virgin's name was Mary. And he came to her and said, "Greetings, favored one! The Lord is with you. But she was much perplexed by his words and pondered what sort of greeting this might be. The angel said to her, "Do not be afraid, Mary, for you have found favor with God. And now, you will conceive in your womb and bear a son, and you will name him Jesus. He will be great and will be called the Son of the Most High, and the Lord God will give to him the throne of his ancestor David . . . Mary said to the angel, "How can this be, since I am a virgin?" The angel said to her, "The Holy Spirit will come upon you and the power of the Most High will overshadow you; therefore the child to be born will be holy; he will be called the Son of God. And now your relative Elizabeth in her old age has also conceived a son; and this is the sixth month for her who was said to be barren. For nothing will be impossible with God." Then Mary said, "Here am I, the servant of the Lord; let it be with me according to your word." Then the angel departed from her (Luke 1:26–38).

Our highest activity must be response, not initiative.[1]

L ET US IMAGINE A devout first-century Jewish maiden at her prayers as she is suddenly visited by an angel of the Lord. If we are aware of the Old Testament back story, we can enter even more pointedly into the climactic nature of this moment. So let us hear the echo of Sarah's angelic visitation that ends in laughter, pregnancy, and Isaac's birth. Let us remember Samuel's surprising birth to Hannah after many faithful yet

1. Lewis, *The Problem of Pain*, 51.

9

barren years. Don't forget Rachel's humiliating wait for a child that ends in the gladness of Joseph's birth. All these help us penetrate further into this text. Even more intimately connected is the birth of Moses, the liberator of Israel. Remember, Moses is at once hidden and vulnerable, both in the bulrushes of the Nile and growing up in Pharaoh's own household. At his birth and during many times to come, he barely survives the violence of empire. All together these stories disclose a God-breathed conspiracy awaiting the climax that is Mary's story.

To recognize this long train of surprising and vulnerable births helps us overcome a "primary impulse" to glibly reduce this story as a plea to put Christ (or in this case, Mary) back into Christmas. An awareness of the back story offers more than further material for a devotional attitude as opposed to a skeptical approach to the text. Frankly, there is too much evidence that religious readers are as guilty of "maintaining and aggrandizing the self" as the skeptical. The experiment I am proposing is an equal opportunity agenda for unbelievers, believers, and those somewhere in between to break free of a whole variety of inattentive readings.

Of course, there is risk involved in paying fresh attention. Each fresh immersion, modest though it is, may involve us in a "temporary annihilation" that has a kind of congruence with Mary's provisional bereavement, for the divine appointment announces the time has come to let go of her dreams of how God shall meet her in exchange for an openness to God's surprise, where the annihilation of self bears fruit in finding it again beyond both hope and fear.

ENLIGHTENED MISREADINGS

This experiment in reading assumes that both the religious and the skeptical quite often read without much risk or without paying too close attention. Before we consider how religious readers distract themselves, let us consider an approach that for several centuries now has inhibited our mental and emotional receptivity. I refer to the Enlightenment reading habit in which both the many moderately educated readers and the few highly educated have been trained to view the birth narratives in Luke and Matthew as historically *incredible* and to put it bluntly, to view traditional Christianity as based on a mistake.[2] According to this view, Jesus actually came to teach certain timeless truths, but these were soon obfuscated

2. See Wright, *Judas and the Gospel of Jesus*, 120ff.

by the church, as it both naively and connivingly corrupted the original message, ornamenting it with stories of miracles, angelic visitations, and apocalyptic endings, all the while seeking to control and profit by the message's distribution.

Behind this reading is a preliminary bias: that the Christian story as it stands, including the miraculous aspects of the birth narrative, is an incoherent pastiche of historical impossibilities. Such a way of reading refuses to suspend disbelief long enough to hear the story as it was meant to be heard with its historical truth claim intact. Lewis names this philosophical bias "naturalism," challenges its internal coherence, and asks careful readers to set it aside and to grant the Christian story the courtesy of listening to it in its native context, including the awkward claim to historical truth.[3]

Hence the first step for the skeptical reader who will risk a "temporary annihilation" of the reading self is to identify the Enlightenment paradigm that filters the text. Having identified the filter, we may choose, as Coleridge would say, to suspend our disbelief in order to properly receive the text itself.[4] When skeptics venture beyond their Enlightenment comfort zones, they may find not an arbitrary and confusing divine intrusion but a pattern of healing intervention, through a deeply personal gift to ones specially chosen to bear these weighty honors for the sake of others.

POP CULTURE MISREADINGS

A lack of attention to what is actually going on in the text explains why "the many" need to jazz up Mary's story. Some enliven the story with a fresh coat of meaning by ingeniously attaching its outer form to new inner content. Recall how four decades ago the Beatles revisited Mary's reply to the angel, "Let it be." The familiar words became a calming refrain for a new generation, a plea to discover a "peaceful, easy feeling" amidst a tension-filled world of Cuban missile crises, assassinations, and the Vietnam War. However, this mood remix transferred Mary's words from her original Jewish context and inserted them into the *world-renouncing* Eastern vision of the world as *Maya*, the veil of illusion, a not unlikely description of the Vietnam War era for many listeners of popular music. And *voila!* The wisdom of Mary became an accompanying mantra for the

3. Lewis, *Miracles*, 84.

4. Coleridge, *Biographia Literaria*, chapter XIV.

radical priest/guru who advises people to "tune in, turn on, drop out." Later, George Harrison's embrace of Hinduism was overt in the Hindu/Pantheist anthem, "My Sweet Lord." But the process of transplanting old Christian idioms into new religious contexts had been at work for some time. So let Mary's wisdom be . . . Buddhism's *world-renouncing* strategy of non-attachment? Yes, but only if you set aside the *world-embracing* covenant of Yahweh with Israel, the first-century Jewish captivity under Imperial Rome, and Mary's willingness to join God's plan to ransom even more than captive Israel, for God's intent to ransom will include the *entire creation through* Israel, through Mary and her child. However, give the Beatles their due. The original drama has been so often misread by the pious, one can hardly fault the minimally churched for attempting to retrieve a morsel of meaning from one more tired Western tradition.

PIOUS MISREADINGS: THE DOMESTICATED CHRISTMAS

I don't wish to sound harsh about two thousand years of Church tradition in what I am going to say next. Full credit to the Church for preserving Mary's words. But Christians have a nearly insatiable appetite (supplied by compliant preachers) for substitute feeling-contexts to awaken our drifting attention to the actual story. For well past a century now, the Church has leaned heavily on an alternative mood to the one actually imbedded in the birth narrative. It is no accident that nearly all the children's Christmas pageants omit any reference to Mary's questions, Joseph's plans for a secret divorce, and Herod's response to the news.[5] Why so? It would "destroy the mood." Which mood is this? Why, the nostalgic scene of family and friends gathered round a fireplace, not a manger, where gifts are offered, not to Jesus, but to one another. Also AWOL are frankincense and myrrh, though a bag of gold to pay for all these gifts would be nice. The sole angel in residence is the one perched atop an evergreen tree elegantly mounted in the living room. Crown it all with the presence of small children singing carols (or nostalgic remembrances thereof) and behold how thoroughly we have morphed Mary's *Magnificat* into a hymn to domestic *gemütlichkeit* (cosiness).

There are a number of historical trends that have formed our now indigenously Westernized Christmas scenario. Karl Barth identified nineteenth-century father of German liberal theology, Friedrich

---

5. A glorious exception is Robinson, *The Best Christmas Pageant Ever.*

Schleiermacher, as a passionate admirer and advocate of the family domestic Christmas. Schleiermacher endorsed the domestic family mood
around the tree as the best way *into* the birth narrative! He paid special
tribute to the piety of his little daughter, Sophie, whose innocent singing
of hymns captured for him the essential serenity at the heart of Christmas.
The story of Mary, he says, is the storycloth that swaddles the elevation of
our humanity; the birth of Christ symbolizes the birth of *our* deepened
awareness.[6] But if *indwelling* describes the manner in which the reader
receives the atmosphere *intrinsic to the text*, what shall we call this cozy
blanketing of Luke with a nineteenth-century Prussian (and in England,
Victorian) Christmas domesticity? For an accurate mood awareness, one
would far better start with an artist contemporary to Schleiermacher, the
Pre-Raphaelite, Dante Gabriel Rosetti, and his work, *The Annunciation*.
Rosetti takes the risk of entering Mary's new upside down world and
paints what he sees when he goes there: the intensity, the recoiling, indeed the terror of that moment.[7] From out of this inner wrestling with the
angel, Mary's response emerges.

REVERENT MISREADINGS: EMBALMING THE TEXT

Schleiermacher illustrates how often the church is better at embalming
Mary's story than remembering it. Hence come the various make-up art-
ists: the Enlightenment touchup, the popular music re-imaging, and the
"family values" restoration themes all rise forth to restore meaning. By
embalming I mean that when we bring an *a priori* notion of reverence
for Mary or the text (probably both), we paradoxically cut ourselves off
from the text's intrinsic emotion and so must instead rely on an emotional
artifice transplanted from elsewhere. The church's advent mood becomes
dependent on a prepackaged Christmas sentiment. Lest we tarnish the
halos painted onto the text, we airbrush away whatever interferes with
this "all is calm" mood we are imposing, especially Mary's fear, confusion,
and questioning of God. Though Mary's genuine anguish (not to mention
Joseph's) is central to the plot, we silence them because our preferred way
of reverencing Mary ignores her human dilemma. It is no surprise, then,

---

6. Quoted by Barth, "Schleiermacher's Celebration of Christmas," 154. For further
reflections on Schleiermacher's interpretation, both its extraordinary appeal as well as
critical questions, see Begbie, *Resounding Truth*, 141–8.

7. http://www.rossettiarchive.org/zoom/s44.img.html.

that when we begin to ask questions of applying the text to ourselves, we have already gone quite far in training ourselves to mute, fast forward, or *docetize* any angel debates of our own.

Devotional readers embalm the story in other ways. Sometimes we are so anxious to affirm the proper doctrine about this story that we obsess on defending the creed rather than receiving the meaning afresh. But when we read a text in order to protect it or convert other readers to its message, we disconnect ourselves from Mary's felt response recorded therein, as well as the other recipients whose lives were forever changed by the events. Thus the *meaning* of the story mutates into crafting apologetics for the virgin birth, not receiving the story, including Mary's fears and questions, not including the doubts and fears within the hearts of even the most orthodox of contemporary readers. However, a fresh immersion into Mary's fear and questioning might awaken our own. This entails an emotional risk on our part.

What happens when we use the text as a litmus test to separate believers from nonbelievers? I suggest this only produces an inner competition between anxiety and serenity. Those who take the story as God-given are our people (serenity); the rest are against us, Mary, even God (anxiety). This gaining and losing of team members is the heavy price of reading defensively. But when I use the story to divide believers from doubters, I have missed the way the story actually unites us in a communion of astonished *listening*. The purpose of the story was never to set Mary *against* her fellow creatures, particularly all skeptical non-admirers, but rather to show how God came to be Emmanuel, God with (all of) us. As the story proceeds, Mary will find herself amidst all manner of sinful types—religious, nonreligious, and shades in between. My point is that polemical religious reading turns Mary's unique divine/human encounter into a checklist for identifying who is in the kingdom and who is not. This reading makes no demands for bereavement or self-annihilation. It easily slips into a reading for a comforting victory over one's theological opponents.

RESPONSE AND RESPONSIBILITY

The above is preliminary for examining how religious or pious reading can seriously avoid a more radical indwelling of the text. To offer a parable of such misreading, I call upon the long-running national public radio program created by Garrison Keillor, *The Prairie Home Companion*, and his regular feature of news from Lake Wobegon, a fictional but based-on-fact hometown, "Where all the women are strong, the men are good looking and all the children are above average."[8] Listeners are aware that Wobegon is quite a churchy place, where an array of denominations and clergy helps people practice the art of responsible living. For our purposes, I focus on the Catholics, led (or commanded) by Father Emil. Do you recall the church's name? *Our Lady of Perpetual Responsibility*. In the confession box, Father Emil can be heard to sternly mutter now and again, "Oh, you didn't? Shame on you!" We chuckle at such heavy handedness and pity his scolded flock, but how does one teach responsibility to an irresponsible culture? With Father Emil, at least you get boundaries. You know you ought to behave responsibly, for heaven's sake!

What can possibly be the connection between Mary's response to the angel and a church named "Our Lady of Perpetual Responsibility"? What does this abstract noun "responsibility" have to do with the active verb "respond" as in the art of responding well to a text, or to an angel? Lewis and his friend Owen Barfield loved to excavate the history of words in order to recover meanings that the sands of time and cultural practice had worn away. Their example, plus the juxtaposition of twinned words inspired by Jane Austen (such as *Pride and Prejudice* and *Sense and Sensibility*) prompted me to explore the Oxford English Dictionary (OED) for possible clues about the relationship between *response* and *responsibility*. Might the history of word usage unearth a clue about religious misreadings, as evidenced by the descent from Mary's magnificent *response* to Father Emil's parish full of perpetual *responsibility*?

What I discovered was that *response* first came into English from Latin in the fourteenth century, where its first recorded use occurs in, of all places, church, and refers to *the reply* of the congregation to a verse of Scripture spoken or sung by the priest. It's that part of the liturgy said or sung by the people *in response*. Moving along a century, *respond* is used to refer to the one half pillar attached to a wall to support an arch. The pillar on the other wall across the sanctuary? That's a *corresponding* pillar. "*To answer. To reciprocate. To act in reply to some influence. A response.*" Next question: when does the noun *responsibility* first appear in English? Not until 1643, *over two hundred years later*, when it refers to being accountable to another, and has acquired a moral overtone. Not until 1796, four

---

8. Keillor, *Lake Wobegon Days.*

hundred years later, does it refer to doing one's duty or performing an obligation for which one is *responsible*.[9] I was struck by the historical lag between response and responsibility and how late had come a stress on ethical obligation. However, once the moral admonishment was sounded, it soon dominated the scene. Throughout the Victorian era, *responsibility* came to be used with increasing frequency, urgently reminding readers of their personal moral duty.

What happened? Semantically speaking, meaning migrated from a sung dialogue and worship framework to a legal or moral frame of reference; from a glad response to God's initiative to warnings of reward and punishment. We have camped inside a small strip of meaning within an emphasis on personal, moral liability ever since. I suspect no publishers have on their book lists *The Joy of Responsibility*.

This glimpse into the history of word use offers evidence that the sparking gap between divine and human agency has become for moderns and post-moderns an ugly ditch, either a deterministic causation or a problematic legal obligation. The original pattern of enlivening gift and glad response that Mary felt in her deepest depths has vanished.

Now fast forward to perhaps the defining problem of the Reformation era. I have in mind the tortured struggle of Martin Luther and his search for a merciful God. So perpetually *responsible*, so anxious to please God, this first-born, monk-trained scholar was unable to *respond* to the gracious news to which Mary submitted. Luther, by contrast, steeled himself to bear responsibility for yet another round of confession, contrition, and restitution, as decreed by the church's penitential framework, which he had dutifully internalized. History records that Luther eventually found his way to a free response to grace, far too free for some contemporary critics.[10] How did he come to exchange the onus of *responsibility* that perpetually condemned him for a joyful *response* to God's gracious welcome?

Restoring the "Real Potency"

There is a connection between Luther's crisis and the childhood crisis of C. S. Lewis four centuries later. It hides within the question, "How did

9. *The Compact Oxford English Dictionary*, vol. II, 2513, 2514.

10. In his analysis of early Protestant literature, Lewis reports how loyal Catholics such as Thomas More believed Luther made converts because "he spiced all the poison" with "libertee." Protestant teachings "were not too grim, but too glad to be true." Lewis, *English Literature in the Sixteenth Century*, 34.

Lewis come to write the Narnian Chronicles?" Lewis's answer casts a flood of light on both his own and Luther's crisis. He writes:

> I thought I saw how stories of this kind could steal past a certain inhibition which had paralyzed much of my own religion in childhood. Why did one find it so hard to feel as one was told one ought to feel about God or about the sufferings of Christ? I thought the chief reason was that one was told one ought to. An obligation to feel can freeze feelings. And reverence itself did harm. The whole subject was associated with lowered voices; almost as if it were something medical. But supposing that by casting all these things into an imaginary world, stripping them of their stained-glass and Sunday school associations, one could make them for the first time appear in their real potency? Could one not thus steal past those watchful dragons? I thought one could.[11]

Better than any explanation of the church historians, Lewis lays bare Luther's distortion: the *obligation* to love God paradoxically cuts off our capacity to respond to God's love. Possibly some kind of protest movement must occur in every Sunday school class, every stained glass institution. If not, the children of the righteous will respond—not to the gospel, but to elder brother exhortations about responsibility: "You *should* believe. You *ought* to be thankful to God." The pedagogues of piety rarely notice they have turned the gospel upside down, making *should* news out of *good* news.

Whenever church transposes the *respond* into an initiative, it freezes the emotional response because one cannot *feel* gratitude at the same moment one is told one *ought* to be grateful. Why not? Because the "ought" of *responsibility* centers me on myself, *my* response, and thus diverts attention from the reality that evokes a free *response*. When I focus on how I ought to respond, I have ceased attending to the angel's news. Herein lies the perennial temptation that threatens all devotional reading of Scripture. But Lewis, the master reader, slips us past the *should news* and re-connects us to *good news*. How? By engaging our imaginations, Lewis has smuggled a generation of Narnian readers past the watchful dragons of self-centered devotional reading.

Of course, recent best-selling fiction, heavy with religious overtones, such as *The Da Vinci Code* and the *Left Behind* series, also engage our

---

11. Lewis, "Sometimes Fairy Stories May Say Best What's To Be Said," 37.

imaginations.[12] But this kind of imaginative "use" of the Christian story is like the Englishman searching for a cup of tea on a continental holiday. They have not done the *a priori* work of disengaging from other controlling narratives *before* listening to the gospel. Quite the contrary, they transplant other dominant themes from outside the text and rearrange New Testament events, persons, and church history to lend a verisimilitude to the gospel. Familiar names and syntax springboard readers into a far different story line, the former generated from Gnostic conspiracy theories, the latter from the end-times secrets discovered by nineteenth-century dispensationalist speculations. Trading on such resemblances, readers imagine they have discovered through these new authors (authorities) the real meaning (and exciting, hidden narrative) behind the official story of Christianity. The story that fascinates me is really about Dan Brown and I, or LaHaye/Jenkins and I, who have read between the lines with the correctly cryptic theological key, uncovering the secrets of history now unfolding before our very eyes. I am an initiate, one of the chosen, who now grasps the meaning behind the externals of traditional churches, governments, and even current Middle Eastern politics.

My point here is not to deny that there may be moral or spiritual insights one can acquire from novel renderings of the gospel. Lewis once wrote: "I suspect that men have sometimes derived more spiritual sustenance from myths they did not believe than from the religion they professed."[13] If one can feed on various myths and derive a measure of spiritual benefit, then a case can be made for some degree of spiritual nutrition in the Rapture novels of Jenkins/LaHaye or the Gnostic conspiracies of Dan Brown. But the rewards and the reading habits they engender are not the same as that granted the reader who *indwells* the original story. I am afraid the nourishment they provide is of the junk food variety, high on fats, low on nutrition. For many readers, such a diet may inoculate them from a response to the real gospel.

Having indicted both the liberal Dan Brown and the conservatives Jenkins/LaHaye with misreading the gospel reminds me they both swim in the same contemporary cultural stream, one that is highly sensitive to self and reader, including the reader's constructions, locations, and responses, not to mention marketing niches. Readers (and authors) have never been

---

12. Cf. Brown, *The Da Vinci Code*. LaHaye and Jenkins, *Left Behind*.

13. Lewis, *God in the Dock*, 67.

more aware of their own agendas. This raises the question I have borrowed from Lewis to begin this experiment: is it hopelessly naïve to attempt to read Mary's story on her terms, not ours? To answer emphatically that I hunger to read the text on its own terms is not to devalue my own questions, nor do I wish to suggest that I approach the gospel with a blank slate or without prior understandings (*vorverstehen*). Let us acknowledge it is an act of faith, to declare openly that it is possible to lay aside our own agendas and submit ourselves to Mary's story in a way that listens to the text's agenda, because we are not content simply to impose our own religious preferences or relentlessly demand novelty. This way of confessing my hope that such a recovery is possible reflects the old paradox at the heart of good reading, namely, "He that loseth his life shall save it."[14]

Rather than trade on familiar words, names, and associations to create a new meaning, Lewis's *The Chronicles of Narnia* offer a real alternative: he clothes the old gospel story in an unexpected garment (fairy tale or *Märchen*) in order to steal past our self-invasive reading habits. In other words (and here I borrow the language of my daughter, Marilee), Lewis costumes the gospel within a non-religious genre and thereby circumvents the pious readers' habit of turning the gospel into a story about ourselves, whether as self-condemning judgment (the early Luther), self-congratulatory religiosity (the Pharisee in every religious culture and century), or initiates with privileged access to a well-kept secret (the Gnostic impulse from Nag Hammadi to Dan Brown to Jenkins/La Haye).

INDWELLING THE ANNUNCIATION TEXT

The broad and much-traveled highways of misreading stand in contrast to the narrow path of indwelling the text. And though context transplants and imaginative intrusions are ever popular, they miss the point of entering into another place and way of life that we could encounter if we opened ourselves to the native country before us. Fortunately, we have a humble tool to keep us from wandering satisfied too long within our own interiority. The *feeling intellect* embodies the way of indwelling that constitutes the essence of good reading. Its way is to listen attentively and obediently to the text within its historical setting. It is *a process that involves a double movement* of emptying ourselves of other dominant narratives and paradigms, and then opening ourselves radically to fresh

---

14. Lewis, *An Experiment in Criticism*, 138.

investigation of the original context, including its religious, historical, social, and literary background. In, with, and under this fresh immersion into text and context, the feeling intellect awakens us to the *ideas* and *emotions* embedded within.

We began this chapter by reading Mary's story against the framework of surprising birth stories throughout Israel's long history. Let us end by engaging the political/cultural layer of first-century background. After all, the Annunciation is spoken from within the world of first-century Judaism, to a people humiliated and suppressed by Imperial Rome, conflicted by fierce religio/political rivalries, torn by competing responses to their occupation, and desperate for deliverance. Amidst this context of brutal occupation and fratricidal conflict, a young Jewish woman enters the scene and by her own quality of response, invites us to set aside all prearranged halos and imaginatively participate in her actual process of trust.

When the text says, *as it does*, that Mary "was *deeply troubled* by what the angel said and *wondered* what this greeting could mean" (Luke 1:29, emphasis added), and further, that she apparently needed the reassuring words, "Do not be *afraid*, Mary" (Luke 1:30, emphasis added), then we should awaken to something deeply troubling as she faces a string of impossibly difficult questions. Moreover, the whole mood is climaxed by an urgent plea, perhaps tinged with confusion and grief, for further clarification: *"How can this be?"* (Luke 1:34). How ironic that the very question skeptics of the birth narrative often ask dismissively and that the religious reader is tempted to devoutly (or docetically) skim past, Mary herself asked first and most passionately. As we are caught up in this awareness, we now begin to pass the Beowulf test of immersing ourselves in felt attunement to the story. Mary's words suggest both the grief of bereavement over a life arrangement now shattered and hope against hope rising to reassemble the broken.

DIVINE PEDAGOGY

Religious educators like myself are trained to think in terms of learning outcomes. If I ask, "Through all of this, what did God hope to teach Mary?" I could answer that God chose her to be the first witness to this good news and that God wanted her to *respond well*. If I suggest as a corollary that God was teaching Mary *responsibility*, it raises further questions about God's pedagogical strategy. Just how did God teach her *responsibility*? The answer begins with a costly gift given. To receive it properly suggests a costly reception. That is, God first gives that which is profound and precious beyond explanation, which in turn evokes in Mary a *correspondingly* costly response. Luke's text catches Mary in the process of bereavement over what can never be and in the movement toward hope over what may now come, beyond all human expectations.

The story hints that the cost to Mary will escalate. Just for starters, by receiving the gift, Mary will be regarded as an immoral woman, a sinner, perhaps forfeiting her life. (Immoral women were subject to execution by stoning in first-century Jewish culture.) If we wondered why Joseph takes Mary along to register (pay taxes) in Bethlehem, it is probable he's not sure what might happen to her should he leave her behind.[15] Beyond the routine courage of raising a peasant family, there will now be leveraged the pressing flight to Egypt and the insecure status of a refugee on foreign soil. This is only the beginning. Simeon's dark blessing spoken over Mary frames Jesus and Mary's journey within a stark prophecy: "This child is destined for the falling and the rising of many in Israel, and to be a sign that will be opposed so that the inner thoughts of many will be revealed— and a sword will pierce your own soul too" (Luke 2:34–35).

When Mary says *let it be,* she agrees to be caught up in this enormously costly restoration. Readers who tune into Simeon's dark prophecy understand why Lewis once described this atmosphere as "very militant; the hero, the 'judge' or champion or giant-killer, who was to fight and beat death, hell and the devils, had at last arrived . . ."[16] Dorothy Sayers, one well acquainted with the feeling intellect as both reader and author, describes the gospel story as *terrifying.*[17] It was J. R. R. Tolkien who coined the term *eucatastrophe* (good catastrophe) to depict the atmosphere of this tragic-yet-healing event of world history.[18] He further notes (perhaps having his formerly atheist friend Lewis in mind) that many skeptical readers have come to accept it as true *on its own terms.* Yet for the past three hundred years the Enlightenment framework now native to Western culture has

---

15. I am indebted to the work of Kenneth Bailey, whose reconstructive explorations into the first-century world of the New Testament have been fittingly described by N. T. Wright as "eyes to the blind." Wright, *Jesus and the Victory of God,* 129. For the above reflections, see Bailey, *Jesus Through Middle Eastern Eyes,* 46.

16. Lewis, *Reflections on the Psalms,* 104–5.

17. Sayers, "The Dogma Is the Drama," 24.

18. Tolkien, "On Fairy Stories," 72.

made it far more complicated to read Mary's story with this *felt awareness* advocated by Lewis, Sayers, and Tolkien, much more than even reading *Beowulf* with the proper atmosphere of implicit terror.

As Luke's gospel proceeds, the atmosphere of danger mounts. Herod's jealousy launches an attack upon the village as a "nick of time" dream arouses Joseph to departure. Another dream, this time the Magi's, warns them to avoid Jerusalem and Herod and take a circuitous return home in order to buy the refugees precious time to escape. The emotion surrounding this narrative is nothing like Schleiermacher's Prussian family Christmas gathered 'round the decorated living room tree, pondering the innocent piety of children. More emotionally congruent is the hurried departure of Frodo Baggins in Tolkien's *The Lord of the Rings*:

> For it seems to me that you have set out only just in time, if indeed you are in time. You must now make haste, and neither stay nor turn back; for the Shire is no longer any protection to you.[19]

Echoing Luke's distant *evangelium*, Bilbo's birthday celebration vertiginously careens from joy to doom as black riders scour the Shire, seeking to destroy the Ringbearer before he threatens their power. Tolkien, of course, has confessed his belief that the writer of a good fairy tale effoliates the tale of the one great catastrophe (*eucatastrophe*), which has in the gospel incarnated itself in history, space, and time.[20] Echoes of a deadly but hope-filled birth frame the recent runaway best-selling Harry Potter series by J. K. Rowling. Once again, a mood of *terror, grief, and hope against hope* is roused in us by the survival of infant Harry, even though the vicious attack of Lord Voldemort claims both his parents. This dark but hopeful launch sets the stage for the inevitable replay of Harry's initial encounter, yet offers hope that somehow Potter will be up to the task. Meanwhile, in the cold prose of human history and Luke's gospel, Mary, Joseph, and the child slip quietly out of Bethlehem to sojourn in Egypt, till Herod's time is up.[21]

19. Tolkien, *The Lord of the Rings*, 97.

20. Tolkien, "On Fairy Stories," 71–2.

21. Once more a Pre-Raphaelite painter, this time Holman Hunt, has penetrated into the emotion embedded within the gospel narrative of the flight to Egypt. According to John Ruskin, Hunt's painting "Triumph of the Innocents" (1875) was the most significant religious painting of its time. Cf. Ruskin, v.33, 277.

CONTEMPORARY READER RESPONSE

Having read this far, I doubt the reader will expect that *indwelling* the text will spit out fast answers about applying this text for today's readers. Hopefully this chapter of prolegomena might rein in the habit of inattentive wandering off along the byways of importing meanings and moods that divert us from the ever-strange, ever-new text before us. So where have we got to thus far? While it is true that this story about Mary's response ought to arouse an echo in us when we read it today, it is even more true to see that Mary is far more than a good example who teaches post-modern readers the meaning of submission. This text claims to be *for us* the singular moment in history when the highly favored one and none other has been prophesied over. This unmarried young woman now throws her lot in as the handmaid of this project and kneels, turning herself toward this turning point in human history as through her, Israel's long story (with its history of unlikely birth stories, from Sara to Hannah to Rachel) finds fulfillment at last.

The ripple effect of this defining nativity propels further unexpected beginnings. Still to come is the unlikely birth of the church recorded by Luke in volume two of his narrative, where on Pentecost, despite every resistance, the Holy Spirit descends upon a fractured and fractious people. There at last they finally learn how to pray together as one body though having many members. The unlikely birth of the church sets in motion one more new beginning, which points toward both a final battle and a final birth. The closing chapters of the New Testament tell of the nativity of the new heaven and new earth, so utterly conclusive it inaugurates the moment when every tear shall be wiped from human eyes.

Of course, it's useless to speculate how much of all this Mary foresaw in the birth of the Christ child. But she sensed she was a partner in something definitive, in a most personal way and yet, as her sung response of *Magnificat* reveals, she was not unaware of the global implications for the whole human family:

> He has shown strength with his arm; He has scattered the proud in the thoughts of their hearts. He has brought down the powerful from their thrones, and lifted up the lowly; he has filled the hungry with good things, and sent the rich away empty. He has helped his servant Israel, in remembrance of his mercy, according to the promise he made to our ancestors, to Abraham and to his descendants forever (Luke 1:51–55).

Some early editor no doubt lobbied to call this *the astonishing news* instead of *the good news!* Speaking as Western Christians at a time full of wars and rumors of protracted wars, in a culture where religion and the public life of nations has been *both* officially divorced since the Enlightenment *and* unequally yoked in malignant partnerships too many to name, we mustn't ignore how Mary's vision joins together God's intention for her personal world *with* the public life of nations. This raises many questions about the mental and spiritual habits that keep these areas either neatly separate on the one hand or falsely wed together on the other. In hopes of remaining open to a response that reflects the global *and* personal sense of Mary's own, let us close with a lone question of contemporary application: might God use this ancient story once again to "scatter the proud, lift up the lowly, fill the hungry with good things, and send the rich away empty"? Indwelling her response, there may come forth a new response in us that connects to the lowly and the hungry—for these are the people Mary carried in her heart as she pondered the gift given. Indwelling her response, we may come to hear and to speak a new warning to all who resist the gift she bears: the proud, the powerful, and the rich. My hope as a reader is this—that having indwelt the text and been changed as a result, I will turn toward the world with *Magnificat* lenses. Having taken a fresh look at the beginning of the gospel story, let us proceed to the climactic narrative.

2

Atonement: Aslan's How (Rom 3–5)

Love's as hard as nails,
Love *is* nails:
Blunt, thick, hammered through
The medial nerves of One
Who, having made us, knew
The thing He had done,
Seeing (with all that is)
Our cross, and His.[1]

We think that Maleldil would not give it up utterly to the Bent One, and there are stories among us that He has taken strange counsel and dared terrible things, wrestling with the Bent One in Thulcandra.[2]

For the wages of sin is death but the gift of God is eternal life through Jesus Christ our Lord. And all are justified by God's free grace alone, through his act of liberation in the person of Christ Jesus. For God designed him to be the means of expiating sin by his death, effective through faith. God meant by this to demonstrate his justice, because in his forbearance he had overlooked the sins of the past (Rom 3:23ff).

A WALK BETWEEN THE WORLDS

In 1931, thirty-three-year-old Lewis writes to his oldest friend, Arthur Greeves, "I have just passed on from believing in God to definitely believing in Christ—in Christianity. I will write about it later. My long night talk with Dyson and Tolkien had a good deal to do with it."[3] In his next

1. Lewis, "Loves as Warm as Tears," 123.

2. Lewis, *Out of the Silent Planet*, 121.

3. Hooper, *They Stand Together*, 425.

letter, Lewis tells Greeves that what had been holding him back from embracing Christianity was the meaning of the death of Jesus. "My puzzle was the whole doctrine of *Redemption*: in what sense the life and death of Christ 'saved' or 'opened salvation to' the world" (emphasis added). Lewis didn't need convincing that the world was a mess or that humanity needed help. "What I couldn't see was how the life and death of Someone Else (whoever he was) two thousand years ago could help us here and now—*except in so far as his example helped us*"[4] (emphasis added). Of course, Lewis understood that mere Christianity saw Jesus as much more than an exemplar, a Jewish Socrates inspiring us to courageous living. "And the example business, tho' true and important, is not Christianity: right in the centre of Christianity, the gospels and St. Paul, you keep on getting something quite different and very mysterious expressed in those phrases I have so often ridiculed ('propitiation'—'sacrifice'—'the blood of the Lamb')—expressions which I could only interpret in senses that seemed to me either silly or shocking."[5]

That evening Dyson and Tolkien proposed something that aroused in Lewis a new connection to Jesus. Though it sounds strange, the breakthrough came when Lewis began to read the accounts of Jesus's death *in the same way* he read pagan stories of sacrifice. After all, he freely admitted to his friends that he was "mysteriously" moved by sacrifice in paganism. As a child, one of his earliest experiences of joy was hearing the words, "I heard the voice cry, Balder the beautiful is dead, is dead."[6] It was the same with "the notion of a dying and reviving God . . . provided I met it anywhere *except* in the Gospels." The difference was the *approach* to pagan stories compared to the gospel story. During this momentous walk, Lewis became aware that he was guilty of some serious misreading. What was missing? *"A certain openness in which I was prepared to feel the myth as profound and suggestive of meanings beyond my grasp even tho' I could not say in cold prose 'what it meant'"* (emphasis added).[7]

Having spoken in a spirit of exploratory friendship with Tolkien and Dyson, Lewis's icy response had finally begun to melt. After this extraor-

4. Gandhi writes, "I could accept Jesus as an . . . embodiment of sacrifice . . . His death on the Cross was a great example to the world, but that there was anything like a mysterious or miraculous virtue in it my heart could not accept." Gandhi, *Autobiography*, 119. One wonders what atonement theology was being taught by Gandhi's Christian missionary friends.

5. Hooper, *They Stand Together*, 427.

6. Lewis, *Surprised by Joy*, 23.

7. Hooper, *They Stand Together*, 427.

dinary conversation, Lewis writes again to Greeves and reports how he has re-read St. Paul's epistle to the Romans and now sees in Paul's writings the same *deeply moving ideas about death* that always touched him in the stories of George MacDonald. What has happened? The *effect* behind pagan myths of sacrifice and death—Balder, Adonis, Bacchus—had now joined to Paul's theology of the divine courtroom and judgment. The deeply moving emotion surrounding death now connects the grim austerity of a courtroom scene ("God meant by this to demonstrate his justice") as all humankind, Jew and Gentile, stand in the dock before the sovereign judge of heaven and earth.

DEEP JUSTICE

Years later, Lewis wrote about a neglected back story to the portrait of divine judgment in Romans.[8] He tells how when the Psalmist ponders the coming day of judgment, there is not a hint of dreaded anticipation. Instead there rises up a longing for it, in which he will be eager to proclaim his innocence and receive his true desserts. "O let the nations rejoice and be glad, for thou shalt judge the folk righteously . . . Judge me, O Lord my God, according to thy righteousness."[9] An observant reader notices the lack of dread on the Psalmist's part, as the writer yearns for his day in court. He yearns for it because he anticipates not a perfection-demanding critic but a *judge* in the sense of a champion, who will rescue the people from the oppressor and reward heavy damages to the injured party. But doesn't this sort of imagined innocence seem flawed from a New Testament perspective? "There is none that is righteous. No not one" (Rom 3:10). Surely a proper evaluation will find us all guilty beyond a shadow of doubt? Surely the Israelite's desire for justice is psychologically naïve, indistinguishable from a longing for revenge? That is, unless we have a witness to a facet of justice that mustn't be omitted when reading St. Paul. Yes, the grimmest of truths must be faced: death is our just dessert. "The wages of sin is death . . ." read on, "but the gift of God is eternal life through Jesus Christ our Lord" (Rom 3:23). Do both parts of the sentence speak of God's justice/righteousness or only one?

In *The Lion, the Witch, and the Wardrobe*, the sulking little brother Edmund offends the deep magic built into the foundations of Narnia.

8. Lewis, *Reflections on the Psalms*, 15.
9. Ibid.

He cruelly betrays his siblings. The deep magic declares that one who betrays another forfeits one's own life. This foundational magic justifies the witch's challenge to Aslan, as she insists the traitor be handed over. When the lion proceeds to negotiate with the witch, he never disputes the magic's rule, but instead offers his own life in exchange for Edmund's. The witch gladly accepts, thinking she has won the upper hand, for once Aslan is eliminated, nothing can stop her from terminating all other claimants to the throne. What the witch does not "see" as she looks at the founding law/magic of Narnia is a deeper law/magic more ancient still. As Aslan later explains:

> But if she could have looked a little further back, into the stillness and the darkness before Time dawned, she would have read there a different incantation. She would have known that when a willing victim who had committed no treachery was killed in a traitor's stead, the Table would crack and Death itself would start working backwards.[10]

By substituting the language of *fairie* and children's story (*magic, incantation*) for the language of the law court (law, justice, desserts), Lewis retells the news of Jesus's death. Set aside is the world of legal transactions and criminal court proceedings in exchange for an environment alive with the emotional immediacy of a child's experience of death and magical intervention. Alternatively, let's turn it around and say that the high art of myth has descended into the cold prose of ancient history, law courts, crime, punishment, and acquittal. In order to translate the emotional truth within the history and prose, Lewis revivifies them with story (myth). Elsewhere he writes:

> The heart of Christianity is a myth which is also a fact. The old myth of the Dying God, without ceasing to be myth, comes down from the heaven of legend and imagination to the earth of history. It happens—at a particular date, in a particular place, followed by definable historical consequences . . . By becoming fact it does not cease to be myth: that is the miracle . . . *To be truly Christian we must both assent to the historical fact and also receive the myth (fact though It has become) with the same imaginative embrace which we accord to all myths. The one is hardly more necessary than the other* (emphasis added).[11]

10. Lewis, *The Lion, the Witch, and the Wardrobe*, 148
11. Lewis, "Myth Became Fact," 67.

What had shut down Lewis's feeling intellect from probing further into things "profound and suggestive of meanings beyond my grasp"? I suggest it had to do with the doctrinal packaging that surrounded the narrative of Jesus's death. Until Lewis re-read the gospels with the lenses suggested by Tolkien and Dyson, Paul's language of law courts and justice had been formalized into a Western atonement tradition that had rigidified meaning into something that was for Lewis either "silly or nonsense."

What theory is responsible for this crisis in meaning? Writing for those who are exploring *Mere Christianity*, Lewis rarely points the finger at one misconstruction. However, his Scottish mentor, George MacDonald, is less reticent. Over several generations, the teachings of Calvin, the Genevan Reformer, morphed into *Calvinism*, an evolutionary process not without a parallel to *law and legalism*. To MacDonald's mind, this transition had sown many tares alongside the gospel seed to infect the harvest. He singled out the American Puritan, Jonathan Edwards, because he "thinks of the father of souls as if he had abdicated his fatherhood for their sins, and assumed the judge. If he put off his fatherhood, which he cannot do, for it is an eternal fact, he puts off with it all relation to us."[12] After talking with Tolkien and Dyson, Lewis glimpsed the self-giving Father hidden behind the legal robes of Edwards's Divine Judge.

John Macleod Campbell, MacDonald's Scottish contemporary, particularly challenged Edwards's teaching that on the cross, God the Father punished Jesus and did so *with an equivalent punishment* to the greatness of the divine majesty so dishonored in human sin.[13] Bluntly, on the cross Edwards claims that Jesus was punished and tortured by his Father. Edwards is not simply an innovator here, however, for something akin to this notion antedates the Calvinists. Anselm of Canterbury described the work of Christ in a way molded by the language of legal transaction and power (the son's life is of infinite weight, enough to outweigh the enormous weight of sin).[14] Even as friendly a critic of Anselm as Colin Gunton acknowledges that to see Jesus as primarily the victim of divine punishment turns the *metaphor* of divine punishment into a literal, personal action of God upon Jesus in a way that creates a disturbing gulf between

12. MacDonald, *Unspoken Sermons*, series 3, 160–1. "From all copies of Jonathan Edwards' portrait of God, however faded by time, however softened by the use of less glaring pigments, I turn with loathing."

13. Quoted in Campbell, *The Nature of the Atonement*, 119.

14. Gunton, *The Actuality of the Atonement*, 92ff.

the action of God and the action of Jesus.[15] The stress on just punishment points either to an angry Divine Judge or one whose offended grandeur demands a kill to appease his honor. MacDonald found this image of a God of offended dignity so repulsive he never ceased to challenge it in both sermons and novels. God's fatherhood, he says, is the foundation out of which his judgment proceeds. God's judgments are *always* fatherly. As McCloud Campbell puts it, our *filial* link to God is always prior to the judicial.[16]

Thomas Smail has written that to the degree Anselm describes God as primarily one who requires satisfaction and Calvin as one who primarily imposes punishment, doctrinal and pastoral disaster await. To set the compassion of Jesus against the stern judgment of his Father both jeopardizes the unity of God and attacks a believer's confidence that the Father regards us with the same passion as the Son.

> The result can be that we are left with a cringing guilt-ridden religion which has to hide behind the love of Jesus in order to be saved from the only just contained wrath of an angry God. This image is more fatally potent in much popular evangelical piety than we often recognize and it works untold havoc with people's ability to believe in and accept their sonship.[17]

ROMANS IN REVIEW

Suppose we read the Romans law court passages sensing the glad verdict of a compassionate Father, not an angry judge? Remember that by his own admission, the reason Lewis wrote Narnia was to help readers re-read the New Testament apart from tainted Sunday school paradigms and stained glass associations. Certainly Romans isn't shy about declaring a crisis in the cosmic order: "For the wrath of heaven is revealed against all wickedness . . . Be not deceived, there is none righteous, no not one" (Rom 3:10). But reading Narnia may help us read Romans with the eyes Lewis received that began with his long evening walk.

Nearly as soon as we enter the world of Narnia, we meet one who cold-bloodedly advocates for an eye for an eye, life for a life punitive justice: the White Witch. We see how she eagerly affirms the foundation of

15. Ibid., 165.

16. Campbell, *The Nature of the Atonement*, 76.

17. Smail, *The Forgotten Father*, 118.

the emperor's "deep magic," convinced that it establishes her rights to a kill for every traitor. We see how Edmund's injured pride wants to "to get even" with his siblings, "to show them." We see how the witch claims Edmund's treachery has won her the right to a kill, that his life is forfeit. Aslan seems to accept her rationale for retribution and proposes a way to set aside Edmund's penalty in full compliance. The witch accepts the proposal, presumably because to her way of deep magic (which we might call justice in isolation or *solitaria justitia*), she still gets a kill, one even more satisfying, adding further security to her own power.

However, the witch isn't the scholar she thinks she is. She has profoundly misread the emperor's magic. It is true that Narnia's foundation cannot ignore an action that ignores the built-in incantation/law, but the witch fails to observe there is more to divine justice than a balancing of moral/magical bookkeeping and an urgent need to punish offenders. Give her fair due: she understands that justice cannot be ignored. But in the world of Narnia, as on earth, justice was not meant to stand isolated from mercy. As Lewis says elsewhere, though we may distinguish mercy from justice, we must never separate them. The one tempers the other. At their highest level, they meet and kiss.[18]

Thankfully, Narnia has better theologians than the witch. Mr. Beaver recites for the children a deeper, multi-dimensional vision of justice enshrined in the ancient prophecy:

> Wrong will be right, when Aslan comes in sight,
> At the sound of his roar, sorrows will be no more,
> When he bares his teeth, winter meets its death,
> And when he shakes his mane, we shall have spring again.[19]

Had Mr. Beaver a justice-as-penalty-in-isolation cast of mind (and a talent for doggeral rhyme), he would have said: "*Wrong shall be punished, when Aslan comes among ush'd.*" No, says the beaver, *wrong will be put right!* Restorative righteousness is the justice that inhabits the parables

18. Lewis insists that pardon which doesn't acknowledge the recognition of guilt and the notion of dessert has lost its meaning. That is why he argues that all criminal law must include a recognition that punishment implies just desserts. He objects to what he calls the humanitarian theory of punishment because it eliminates any notion of a sin that deserves punishment. If crime is only a disease that needs a cure, it cannot be pardoned. "Thus mercy detached from justice, grows unmerciful." Lewis, "The Humanitarian Theory of Punishment," *God in the Dock*, 294.

19. Lewis, *The Lion, the Witch, and the Wardrobe*, 75.

of Luke 15. As Kenneth Bailey has shown, this most famous of parables is full of an expectation of punishment: the very act of returning home exhibits a youth costumed in failure, who walks a gauntlet of shaming villagers wagging their heads at the sight of him, in an atmosphere of humiliation and punishment. Were a penal frame to stand as the climax of justice, however, the story would have the son walk all by himself, make an appointment with his father's secretary and wait outside until the offended patriarch agrees to see him and accept his son's offer to become a hired hand, the meritorious first step toward earning re-entry into his father's dominion.[20] Instead, the father sets aside his patriarchal dignity and lifts his cloak so he can run and embrace his son. In so doing, he shares the shame and disgrace. Thus the father transfigures the son's humiliating penalty into a celebration of restoration.

One lone player in the drama criticizes the father, accusing him of injustice. Yet toward this other son, the elder brother, the father *also* intervenes with similar generosity. In each case, the goal of restorative justice is not to punish evil but to heal its victims and make reconciliation possible.

EARLY CHURCH AND NARNIAN JUSTICE

If we set the witch's theory of crime and punishment alongside the lion's, we see that Lewis has us weigh competing notions of justice. To awaken the healing alternative to the attenuated justice of the witch, Lewis takes us back to the early church, to the second-century theologian Irenaeus and his notion of justice as *restoration*, or as he famously described it, *recapitulation*.[21] In this drama of divine justice, the Son of God descends to space and time, and into our humanity, not to be an object of divine wrath so God lets us off the legal hook, but rather to reclaim the entire human journey from birth to death and beyond death, untwisting our disobedience by a healing obedience for the entire human journey, from Mary's womb to the tomb of Joseph of Arimathea. The Son confronts the cosmic pollution from within and applies the healing antidote of a faithful response. That is, God "defeats" evil not by ruthlessly punishing guilty parties but by faithfully untwisting every step of false response with true submission to the Father's will. In *Miracles*, Lewis describes this deep,

---

20. Bailey, *The Cross and the Prodigal*, 54–7.

21. Irenaeus, *Against Heresies*, 446, 448.

restorative justice that he first glimpsed in the long talk with Tolkien and
Dyson, using Irenaeus's signature designation.

> In the Christian story, God descends to re-ascend. He comes
> down; down from the heights of absolute being into time and
> space, down into humanity; down further still, if embryologists are
> right, to *recapitulate* in the womb ancient and pre-human phases
> of life; down to the very roots and seabed of the Nature He has
> created. But He goes down to come up again and bring the whole
> ruined world up with Him. One has the picture of a strong man
> stooping lower and lower to get himself underneath some great
> complicated burden. He must stoop in order to lift, he must almost
> disappear under the load before he incredibly straightens his back
> and marches off with the whole mass swaying on his shoulders. Or
> one may think of a diver first reducing himself to nakedness, then
> glancing in mid-air, then gone with a splash, vanished, rushing
> down through green and warm water into black and cold water,
> down through increasing pressure into the death-like region of
> ooze and slime and old decay; then up again, back to color and
> light, his lungs almost bursting, till suddenly he breaks surface
> again, holding in his hand the dripping, precious thing that he
> went down to recover. He and it are both colored now that they
> have come up into the light: down below, where it lay colorless in
> the dark, he lost his color too.[22]

THE WAGES OF SIN

From his later letters and writings, it seems Lewis came to accept a penal aspect to the meaning of Christ's death. In a sense, the triune God
allowed the consequences of evil (which includes a penal consequence)
to fall on Jesus. MacDonald had taught Lewis that death in itself, or at
least as a fallen creation experiences death, has intrinsically an element
of punishment. With human mind and body no longer harmonious with
the Creator, no longer alive internally as intended, we now tread a self-
destructive path to death, including a punishment for disobedience, as
part of our disgrace of "horror and ignominy."[23] But in the divine alchemy,
our resulting death leads far beyond punishment. Death itself contains a
safety device, for once we have fallen, a natural immortality would only

22. Lewis, *Miracles*, 115–6.
23. Lewis, *Miracles*, 133.

perpetuate pride and lust forever.[24] But this causes a fundamental change in death itself. Because Christ's dying is an act of submission and faith, it is also therefore *an act of mercy.* When Jesus willingly and humbly took our death as punishment upon himself, death's atmosphere was altered irrevocably. From the climate of rebellion, alienation, and punishment, Jesus baptized even death into the self-giving and self-renunciation at the heart of the Holy Trinity. Thus Jesus surrounds even the penal atmosphere of death with a liberating hope.

> Humanity must embrace death freely, submit to it with total humility, drink it to the dregs, and so convert it into that mystical death which is the secret of life. But only a Man who did not need to have been a Man at all unless He had chosen, only one who served in our sad regiment as a volunteer, yet also only one who was perfectly a Man, could perform this perfect dying; and thus (which way you put it is unimportant) either defeat death or redeem it. He tasted death on behalf of all others. He is the representative "Die-er" of the universe: and for that very reason the Resurrection and the life. Or conversely, because He truly lives, He truly dies, for that is the very pattern of reality. Because the higher can descend into the lower He who from all eternity has been incessantly plunging Himself in the blessed death of self-surrender to the Father can also most fully descend into the horrible and (for us) involuntary death of the body. Because Vicariousness is the very idiom of the reality He has created, His death can become ours.[25]

Paul writes: "As in Adam all die, so in Christ, all shall all be made alive" (1 Cor 15:22). In other words, as the poet and preacher John Donne has put it, "death, thou shalt die."[26] For Lewis, death as the wages of sin and as criminal court punishment graphically reveals a facet of the human predicament. But death as *penalty* is but a foothill and not the summit of death's meaning. Jesus's death *includes* punishment, but *mercy* and *safety-device* surround the summit. Most profoundly, Jesus's death expresses the Trinitarian mystery of self-surrender at the heart of divine reality. Edmund's terrible fate is interrupted by the deeper magic of restorative justice at the heart of God.

24. Whether or not Lewis also imbibed this from Irenaeus, the idea goes back to him. Cf. Book III, chapter XXIII. 6 (457).

25. Lewis, *Miracles*, 33ff.

26. Donne, "Death Be Not Proud," 909.

In our moment of greatest need, Jesus's death meets us in an act of sacrificial love. Indeed, Lewis speaks of "being let off because Christ had volunteered to bear a punishment instead of us." But one moment, says Lewis. "If God is prepared to let us off, just do so. Why punish an innocent instead?"[27] If you think of *police court punishment*, Lewis says, yes, it is *silly* or *nonsense*. This is the kind of penal theology that for Lewis only interrupts receptivity to the story. "On the other hand, if you think of a *debt*, there is plenty of point in a person who has some assets paying it on behalf of someone who has not." In other words, "If paying the penalty is not taken in the sense of being punished, but in the more general sense of 'footing the bill' then it is a matter of common experience that, when one person has got himself into a hole, the trouble of getting him out usually falls on a kind friend."[28]

OUR RESPONSE TO CHRIST'S INTERVENTION ALSO NEEDS INTERVENTION

There is something more to death (both Jesus's and ours) that Lewis doesn't want us to miss, and that is how to properly conceive (and imagine) the relationship between divine and human agency. As anyone who has tried to repent knows, it is a tricky business. Our efforts, indeed, our motives, are just not up to the task. In *Mere Christianity*, Lewis describes our debt as being that of rebels against God who need to lay down our arms, surrender, and say we are sorry. Fine, then. Let us tell God we are sorry and give back our wills, even if it means unlearning all the self-conceit and self-will we have been training ourselves in for thousands of years, even if it means undergoing a kind of death, let's get on with it. It will take a bit of work, but at least we can get started on the right road, thank heaven, the path of repentance and surrender.

But Lewis and many others have a problem with this kind of Pelagian, do-it-yourself repentance. To put it simply, repentance cannot be a causal prerequisite of God's forgiveness. Put that way, it becomes the road to legalism and self-righteousness on the one hand, or the road to despair and self-condemnation on the other. Repentance, Lewis writes, "Is not something God demands of you before he will take you back and which He could let you off if he chose; it is simply a description of what going

27. Lewis, "The Perfect Penitent," 59.
28. Ibid., 59.

back to Him is like. If you ask God to take you back without it, you are really asking Him to let you go back without going back."[29]

But if God became a man, says Lewis, then:

> He could surrender his will, and suffer and die, because He was man; and he could do it perfectly because He was God . . . Our attempts at this dying will succeed only if we men *share* in God's dying . . . but we cannot share God's dying unless God dies; and He cannot die except by being a man. That is the sense in which *He pays our debt*, and suffers for us what He himself need not suffer at all (emphasis added).[30]

That's how Jesus pays a debt on our behalf; he does perfectly for us that which we can never do. He pays the debt our rebellious self cannot pay, and in doing so, establishes a beachhead in our humanity for the renewal of our relationship with God.

DAY OF JUDGMENT, DAY OF HOPE?

Before we set aside our Narnian approach to atonement theory, there is one more scene of judgment that will help us join Lewis in a fresh reading of Romans. Eustace Scrubb, through a noxious combination of self-pity, self-indulgence, and disobedience, has turned himself into a little tyrant of a boy. In Narnia he proceeds to get himself turned into a dragon. But this crowning punishment is not the defining feature of his judgment day with Aslan. To be sure, his meeting with Aslan is dreadfully painful. There is a kind of punishment, as Eustace does not escape from facing what he has become. Perhaps the most anguished moment is when Eustace discovers that his situation is utterly beyond self-correction. With tears Eustace rips away at his dragonish scales, but they only reveal more scales. All his efforts at self-cleansing "had been no good."[31] Thus does Eustace's day of judgment contain two conjoined features. The first is the lion's announcement that he cannot cure himself of his dragonish character. But the *punishment* of facing this truth mercifully prepares Eustace to receive

29. Ibid., 60.

30 Ibid. There are some limits in how far to take this illustration. In showing why the incarnation was necessary to pay our debt, Lewis says God needs to help us to do something God in his own nature never does (i.e., "to surrender, to suffer, to submit, to die"). But elsewhere Lewis describes the very interrelations within God, that is, the giving and receiving of love, as a kind of surrendering or dying to self-will.

31. Lewis, The *Voyage of the Dawn Treader*, 95.

the truth that what he can never do for himself, Aslan shall do for him. "Then the lion said—but I don't know if it spoke—You will have to let me undress you. I was afraid of his claws, I can tell you, but I was pretty nearly desperate now. So I just lay flat down on my back to let him do it."[32]

A FINAL COURTROOM SCENE

At the heart of the cosmic order is a justice that does more than simply punish, but restores and recreates. Lewis moves with remarkable consistency along this trajectory first formed at the time of his conversion. His final and most sophisticated novel, *Till We Have Faces*, just happens to end with another courtroom scene of judgment. Here Orual, the proud and wounded queen of Glom, stands before the gods to give account of herself, believing that she has, for love's sake, separated her sister Psyche from her mysterious demon lover/husband. When, beyond all hope, she meets Psyche once more, she discovers the unwelcome truth about her real motivations. I will not go into further details, except to say that whether we call what happens next the punishment of facing the truth or Orual's release from her self-enchantment, the end result, unmistakably, is joy.[33]

Edmund is rescued by a deeper magic. Eustace is cleansed by the lion's claws. Orual is punished by facing the truth about herself, finding an astringent mercy. These mini-narratives are fleeting images glimpsing how Jesus's death and ours are never again to be seen through a penal lens in isolation. None of these descriptions does full justice to a meaning beyond all images and conceptual formulations. That is why Lewis also offers a caution concerning the image of a debt payment: "But remember this is only one more picture. Do not mistake it for the thing itself: and if it does not help you, drop it."[34] After going to the trouble of proposing all these images, why caution us to "drop it" if it doesn't help? Is this theological relativism? Yes, in the sense that Lewis will not impose on his readers what too many zealous preachers imposed on him as they virtually identified their theory of *how* Christ's death saves us with the reality that Christ's death accomplished redemption. Lewis found the punishment-centric theories so appalling, he could not indwell the story.

32. Ibid., 96.

33. For more discussion, see chapter 6 of this present volume.

34. Lewis, *Mere Christianity*, 61.

I conclude that such theories reflect more the witch's magic than that of Narnia's true emperor.

Remember, prior to his coming to faith, Lewis mistakenly thought Christians had to hold a particular lens to the text and view the death of Jesus as God wanting to punish us for our sin but "Christ volunteered to be punished instead, and so God let us off."[35] Many years later, he says he finds this theory less immoral and silly than he used to, but this is faint praise. In order to avoid similar mistakes in the future for himself as well as other teachers of Christian doctrine, he urges us to distinguish between our *theoretical formulations* on the one hand and the *reality* that:

> Christ's death has somehow put us right with God and given us a fresh start. Theories as to *how* it did this are another matter. A good many different theories have been held as to how it works; what all Christians are agreed on is that it does work . . . Theories about Christ's death are not the object of our faith. They are explanations about how it works. Christians would not all agree as to how important these theories are . . . Any theories we build up as to *how* Christ's death did all this are, in my view, quite secondary: mere *plans* or *diagrams* to be left alone if they do not help us, and even if they do help us, not to be confused with *the thing itself.*[36]

Lewis's plea still needs to be heard today. So let us put it simply: No theory of the atonement died for our sins. Jesus did. Thank God for Tolkien and Dyson, who didn't worship at the altar of atonement theories but knelt at the cross. Kneeling there, they invited Lewis to do the same and gave him permission to describe in story, parable, and yes, in repentant theory, "Glimpses of meaning profound and suggestive beyond [human] grasp."

35. Ibid., 57.
36. Ibid., 58–9.

3

Freedom for a Horse, His Boy, and Western Culture
(Or Nurturing Narnians in a Calormen Culture)
(Gal 4)

In the fullness of time, God sent his Son, born of a woman, born under the law, to redeem those under law that we might receive the full rights of sons. Because we are sons, God sent the spirit of his Son into our hearts, the Spirit who calls out "Abba" Father. So you are no longer a slave, but a son; and since you are a son, God has made you also an heir (Gal 4:4–7).

Then Jesus said to the Jews who had believed in him, "If you continue in my word, you are truly my disciples; and you will know the truth and the truth will make you free" (John 8:31–32).

ANCIENT CONTEXT

It may sound shocking that Paul would describe his own people as slaves, but the point is their very reverence for the law as the cornerstone of their uniqueness in the world makes the law function as a guardian power that controls them even as the gentile nations are dominated by various other angels/powers/ principalities.[1]

Of course this theme is not new with Paul. Jesus also likened his own people to slaves. He told those gathered to hear him, "If you continue in my word, you are truly my disciples; and you will know the truth, and the truth will make you free." You can tell he has wounded their pride by their reply: "We are descendants of Abraham and have never been slaves to anyone. What do you mean by saying, 'you will be made free?'" (John 8:31–33). They apparently had forgotten that episode of slavery in Egypt, the ten

1. Cf. Wright, *Paul for Everyone, Galatians and Thessalonians*, 43–7.

northern tribes being shipped off to Assyria, and the remaining tribes of Judah and Benjamin sent packing into Babylon captivity. At that moment they were squirming under the heavy boot of Roman occupation. Never slaves to anyone? There is a correlation between freedom and truth that Abraham's children must never ignore. That connection will continue to shadow all who pursue freedom in isolation from its true partner.

But even as Paul levels his charge, he also makes declaration of liberty. As Isaac was Abraham and Sarah's child of promise, so now in time's fullness Jews and Gentiles are entering a *new Exodus,* a new intimacy with God, disclosed by the special name, *Abba Father.* Naturally, the Jews are more at home with the old Exodus freedom when Moses said to Pharaoh, "Let my people go." They are comfortable with the old stories and customs surrounding the Passover events—the slaughter of the lambs, the daubing of blood on the doorposts, the slaying of the Egyptian firstborn, the escape to the desert, the giving of the law to school them in how to be a people worthy of inhabiting the promised land. Every Jew knows this story of freedom. It is the foundation of their identity as God's people: Moses, Exodus, Law, Covenant. These words *name* the Hebrew people, that is, bestow on them their unique identity in the world—despite the golden calves, the sins of their leaders and kings from Saul to David to Solomon to Rehoboam, despite the apostasy of kings like Ahab and queens like Jezebel, despite even the eventual destruction of Jerusalem and the exile in Babylon. Yes, there was a restoration of sorts under Ezra and Nehemiah, but apart from a brief period of independence during the Maccabean period, Judah remained firmly under foreign powers right down to the current iron-fisted policies of Rome. No wonder they were still awaiting a Messiah, an anointed One, to rid them of their oppressors right up to the moment Mary gave birth to Jesus.

Galatians may well be the earliest document of the New Testament, possibly Paul's first letter. As such it provides a cornerstone interpretation for what the coming of Jesus meant for his own people. Paul applies this new interpretive cornerstone to the foundational story of Israel's slavery and Exodus, except that now, says Paul, the masters are neither the Egyptians nor the Romans so much as "the elements of the world," which he identifies with Israel's slave-like attitude toward the law and its regulations. These mental habits and motivations have kept Israel bound to the past and held her back from God's plan to redeem and reconcile the entire human community as one family, Jews and Gentiles, under the Messiah.

Into this world, Paul announces a new Passover of freedom. This time God sends, not Moses, but his own son, Jesus the Messiah, and through him an enslaved people have finally become children and heirs. Forty days after this new Passover, God shall give, not the law, but the Spirit of his son, to turn the people into true children in their innermost being, not in some outer form of legal, dietary, or racial distinction. The surest evidence this has really happened is that whether they come together or go off alone to pray, there shall arise spontaneously from within an echo of the way Jesus prayed. The Spirit shall move them to call upon God the way Jesus did, using the familiar Aramaic name, *Abba*. We are no longer slaves; we are sons and daughters reconnected to the One after whom every family on earth, Jewish *and* Gentile, receives its name. How then shall we know we are joined together in the same family? The Spirit of Freedom shall grant an inner permission whereby we cry, *"Abba, Father."*

A NEW HUMANISM

If Jesus reveals the truth about God, he also reveals the truth about what it means for humans to be free. We don't hear much in the media these days about humanity as a family of brothers and sisters. We hear quite a lot about humans as citizens of this or that nation state. We hear quite a lot about humans as customers, consumers united in a "global" market. But what is the link between freedom and consumer identity? There is no denying that, on one level, there are corporate identities with assorted logos that link the world together in "free markets." As consumers we are "free" to attach our identities to various product labels. At this level, we relate to one another as customers and clients. Most employers have a department of "human resources," a term that images us as resources for use and inevitably reallocation or possibly disposal as the management sees fit.

But what if these images of identity through nationality, shopping habits, or market resources veil the deepest connection to the truth about human freedom—that we are an interwoven world of cousins, nieces and nephews, siblings, a family with a common Father after whom every family on earth is named (Eph 3:15)? The challenge in the twenty-first century as in the first century is how do we live as freeborn sons and daughters when the dominant culture restricts our true family ties to geographical proximities (the nation state or a tribal/racial subset thereof) or when the culture reduces freedom to consumer choice? How free are we to be truly human when we identify our primary loyalty to class, gender, or racial or ideological identity—and become swept up in the inevitable rivalry for competing resources? These elemental powers and principalities so subtly hold us in thrall. Dwelling amidst this rivalry between nation gods, gender gods, and their competing acolytes, Paul is convinced that this insignificant little movement of which he now belongs—the church, which speaks in many tongues—has birthed our true identity: to live under the logo of one family with one Father revealed by the only begotten Son.

This new identity is vulnerable. Paul warns it is possible to regress to former identities—to live not as sons and daughters but as slaves once more. "Now however, that you have come to know God, or rather to be known by God, how can you turn back again to the weak and beggarly elemental spirits?" (Eph 3:9). It is an awkward fact as old as the Exodus story that under the strains of liberty, people will long for the fleshpots of Egypt. "You foolish Galatians! Who has bewitched you?" Paul asks (Gal 3:1). Invisible habits of slavery can still chain us to the past. If we are surrounded by others with a similar mentality, the risk of infection escalates. In a culture of regression, how shall we retain our freedom?

STUDIES IN WORDS

Now we need to consider some unwelcome evidence about the degree to which a certain kind of slave mindset permeates Western culture. Toward the end of his literary career, Lewis published *Studies in Words*, in which he explores in detail the roots and connections in how over time and cultural pressure the meaning of words develop, shift, and change. He surveys the semantic variations surrounding our English word "freedom" in Greek, Latin, and French. Along the way, he notes the extraordinary ancient contrast in *motivation* between people who were slaves and those who were freeborn. From the writings of the great classical authors, including Aristotle, Plato, Homer, Lucretius, and Tacitus, Lewis assembles the characteristics that make up a slave mentality. It's an interesting and troubling list: slaves are cheeky (a British colloquialism meaning impudent, insolent); they are also shrewd, cunning, up to every trick, determined to look after number one. (It's worth remembering that Lewis is writing in 1961, before the 1980s was labeled a "culture of narcissism.")[2]

2. Cf. Lasch's 1979 classic, *Culture of Narcissism*. Cf. also Ringer's 1977 best-seller,

The stereotypical slave has an axe to grind, an ulterior motive, and is fundamentally lacking in generosity. Aristotle's adjective is "stingy." When a slave-owning society sees a slave without an appointed task, the assumption is he or she will either be flirting, quarrelling, playing dice, or dozing. By contrast, a freeborn person is self-bound by discipline and considers not just her own task at the moment but its implications for the good of the whole. A free person attends to the details in terms of the greater good and vice-versa.[3]

This semantic history permeates the Narnian story, *The Horse and His Boy* where we journey with the slave-minded who discover the true meaning of freedom. We meet Shasta, the young orphan boy, found and raised by a cruel fisherman, brought up in a very hierarchical, slave-holding society. We meet Aravis, in some ways Shasta's opposite number, an aristocratic young lady. But in a society that permits slavery, is anyone truly free? Aravis is running away from home because her father has arranged for her to marry an eligible sub-ruler. But she is not quite "smitten" with a fawning friend of her father's who is three times her age. In Calormen culture, this doesn't matter. He's a good provider of status and financial security. In a slave-owning society, here is the trickledown effect of slavery: the top and the bottom take on slave habits of mind.

The underlying slave mentality is both subtle and pervasive. The freeborn Narnian horses who are escaping with the children have the same identity confusion. One morning when the horse Bree gets up after a very hard ride and decides to have a nice roll in the grass before the saddle goes on, he tells Shasta he should roll in the grass too because it feels so good. Shasta bursts out laughing and says, "You do look funny when you're on your back!" "'I look nothing of the sort,' said Bree." But nevertheless, Bree wonders if rolling in the grass is a proper Narnian thing to do. "'Does it really look funny?' 'Yes it does,' said Shasta, 'but what does it matter?' 'You don't think, do you,' said Bree, 'that it might be a thing talking horses never do—a silly, clownish trick I've learned from

---

Looking Out for Number 1. During the same era, the disciple of Ayn Rand, Alan Greenspan, was appointed chairman of the U. S. Federal Reserve Board (1987–2006), and strove to frame the American economy from 1987 to 2006 within Rand's philosophical foundation: each individual's own happiness is his highest purpose. Selfishness, Rand boldly declared, is a virtue. Cf. Rand, *Atlas Shrugged*.

3. Lewis, *Studies in Words*, 112–4.

the dumb ones? It would be dreadful to find, when I get back to Narnia, that I've picked up a lot of low, bad habits."[4]

This dialogue betrays the worst bad habit of living in a master/slave society, far more troubling than whether or not rolling on your back in the grass is "PC" behavior: Bree and Shasta are perpetually anxious about their true identity and worth. While Shasta yearns to make a good impression, he is quick to feel rejection. He gets red faced when Bree tells of his riding mistakes to Aravis and Hwin. When Aravis hesitates to join in the escape from Calormen, he quickly interprets it as personal rejection: "Why don't you say at once that you think I'm not good enough?"[5] Thus Shasta discloses the daily anguish of the slave-minded.

Of course, an *inferiority* complex instilled by the social order has a reciprocal aristocratic side that also afflicts one's identity. The aristocratic Aravis must undergo a transformation from a *superiority* complex, which threatens to sabotage her and her relationships as surely as Shasta's inferiority worldview bedevils him. Here lies the tragedy of living in a culture that is not really a family but a system of competitive superiors and inferiors; the chains shackle vertically *and* horizontally in a grim dance.

This truth weighed on Nelson Mandela during his long years in prison, long before he became president in South Africa's first democratic election. In his autobiography, he writes how he grew convinced that the whites needed liberation from playing the role of master as much as blacks needed liberation as inferior people.[6] It's a great freedom to no longer have to dominate other people or put one's self above others in order to feel special or alive or valuable within oneself. Like a modern Joseph forgotten in Pharaoh's dungeon, Mandela spent twenty-seven years in prison, not despairing nor indulging in self-pity nor plotting revenge, but preparing to lead a multi-racial democracy of equals. It raises the question I will not answer here: amidst such oppression, how did he acquire (or maintain) a freeborn mind?

In February 2007, a movie was released about the ending of the slave trade in the British Empire, entitled *Amazing Grace*. It's the story of William Wilberforce and other British evangelicals, including the notorious John Newton, former slave trader turned preacher and author of the

---

4. Lewis, *The Horse and His Boy*, 26.

5. Ibid., 33.

6. Mandela, *Long Walk to Freedom*, 624.

famous hymn. It tells how people finally challenged the slavery system and said, "Enough is enough." The economic orthodoxy of the day labeled the Abolitionists as naïve do-gooders. They declared the economic health of the British Empire would be devastated if slavery was simply shut down. The vested interests in maintaining the status quo were, as usual, enormous.

On New Year's Day, 2007, at a commemoration service at Wilberforce's old church in Clapham, the Archbishop of Canterbury, Rowan Williams, went beyond paying tribute to deeds of the past. He declared that we have a twenty-first century form of slavery. Implicit in the design of the international economic system, he said, are massive chains of debt shackling entire nations. The very debt repayment plans function as a means of control and domination whereby Western institutions subjugate the developing world in poverty. He asked: is it possible today for us to feel the same hunger for justice that ended the slave trade by using our freedom for the sake of those whose indebtedness amounts to slavery?[7] Here I rehearse a sample of the statistics of today's economic slavery:

> Prior to the Church-inspired Jubilee campaign of 2000:
> Latin American countries owed over $600 billion.
> Sub-Saharan Africa owed more than $200 billion.
> Mozambique spent four times more in loan interest than health care.
> Zambia five times more on debt than education.[8]

Even the paying of interest on such debt is beyond many nations' abilities. Some have paid back two or three times the original loan, but the debt grows. When a nation like, for example, Mozambique, has paid back five dollars in interest for every dollar it borrowed in the 1960s, and yet according to the debt repayment scheme signed back then, it still owes millions each year to the West just servicing the interest on the debt, millions it cannot invest in health care or education for its own citizens.

Closer to home, there are more disturbing numbers. For instance, as a U. S. citizen, at the time I am writing, over forty-five million of my fellow Americans have no health insurance. To rehearse this statistic may be just another way of distancing, feeling superior, or wringing my hands. How do I begin to be open emotionally to the reality of millions of uninsured citizens, one illness or injury away from financial destitution,

7. Williams, New Year's Message, December 31, 2006.
8. Wright, *The Millennium Myth*, 103–5.

within a nation that paradoxically has the largest economy in the world? How does facing the truth about the marginalization of nearly one out of five Americans set me free? In speaking of "citizens" or statistics about the uninsured, have I colluded in denying the prior reality that I am part of one family, with God our Father and Jesus our brother?

Williams says we need new Wilberforces to say for our generation that the time for ending the third-world debt is long overdue. It is time to face the responsibility for the injuries inflicted upon those we have indebted. It is time to ask how we personally profit from the status quo. It is time we acknowledge that these massive debts form (and deform) all of us who are resigned or perhaps addicted to a world in which debts are not forgiven.

As Mandela reminds us, the chains of slavery tug both ways. There's something damaging our humanity when another person or another country near or far away inhabits this kind of poverty. We are free to be ourselves only when we wake up to the reality behind these numbers and begin to concern ourselves with the good of the whole family, not simply looking out for number one. Today history waits for a new Wilberforce, a new Clarkson, and a Henry Thornton to challenge the slave mentality that for too long has poisoned Western economic and trade policy.

RELEASE FROM THE CAPTIVITY OF SELF-INTEREST

One final symptom of a slave mentality keeps us from freely and without legalism approaching God as *Abba*. The orphan Shasta faces it at the anguishing moment when his comrade Aravis is wounded by a lion. Despite his awkwardness and fear, Shasta intervenes to rescue her, and she ends up safely tended by a 109-year-old hermit! And though both horses are now safe, Aravis now in good hands, Shasta, instead of being safe also and rewarded for a job well done, is given the exhausting task of running on to warn King Lune that the wicked Prince Rabadash of Calormen is fast approaching in a sneak attack. The hermit says, "If you run now, without a moment's rest you will still be in time to warn King Lune."[9] Shasta's heart faints at these words, for he feels his strength utterly depleted. Moreover, he writhes inside at what seems the cruelty of these unfair demands. That's how a slave feels. Lewis the narrator remarks: "He had not yet learned that if you do one good deed your reward usually is to be set to do another

---

9. Lewis, *The Horse and His Boy,* 124.

and harder and better one."[10] These words voice the new heart of a free Narnian waiting to be born.

To his credit, in the teeth of his feelings, Shasta runs on to warn the king—no small task. By good fortune he interrupts the king and his knights on a hunt and succeeds in this unwanted responsibility. But having warned the king, he finds himself once more unrewarded, once again all alone while the king and his soldiers rush off to defend the castle. In their hurried departure, they give Shasta a fresh horse, but he doesn't know how to ride a dumb horse. He's left behind. "'I do think,' said Shasta, 'that I must be the most unfortunate boy that ever lived in the whole world. Everything goes right for everyone except me' . . . And being very tired and having nothing inside him, he felt so sorry for himself that the tears rolled down his cheeks."[11]

At this point in the story, Shasta meets the lion, the unseen presence behind the details of his and everyone's story. The thick fog means he can't see the lion, but he hears its breathing. And when Shasta blurts out, "Who are you?" the lion answers, "One who has waited long for you to speak. Tell me your sorrows." That's enough for Shasta to recite his woes, chapter and verse. As he pours them out one after the other, the lion gives him a perspective that interrupts his self-preoccupied, "looking out for number one" approach to life. The lion speaks and breathes into him a role he now shall play for as long as he partners in healing the wounds of others. Finally he sees what had only been a voice. "The High King above all kings stooped towards him. Its mane, and some strange and solemn perfume that hung about the mane, was all round him. It touched his forehead with its tongue. He lifted his face and their eyes met." And then he vanished.[12]

We began this chapter with Paul's words to the Galatians, "Because we are sons, God sent the spirit of his Son into our hearts, the Spirit who calls out 'Abba' Father." When Shasta hears the voice and looks into the lion's face, he feels the freedom to be who he was intended to be all along. His inferiority feelings, his self-pity, are transposed into a new motivation. He has met the king in whose service is perfect freedom.

---

10. Ibid, 137.
11. Ibid.
12. Ibid., 141.

In reading Galatians 4 and John 8 alongside *The Horse and His Boy*, the feeling intellect grasps how true freedom emerges when we experience our identity as sons and daughters. In meeting with the *Abba* Lion, we experience one who *both* hears our sorrows *and* calls us to mission. By means of such a prayer, Jesus teaches his disciples their true identity as disciples who are learning to stop putting themselves down, to stop the worry about making the right impression. Prayer *to Abba* teaches us to forego the twisted pleasure of self-pity as well as the twisted pleasure of self-conceit.

The need in our day to recover freedom is great because somewhere King Lune needs to be warned and needs to find a lost son. Somewhere the lady Aravis needs a true friend. Of course, it's unfair. How can we possibly accomplish such tasks when we lack the equipment, the resources, the energy? Yet, in prayer to Abba, we are in the presence of the One who, though he was rich, for our sakes became poor. In vulnerable (not performing) prayer, we recover the lost possibility of responding to life as freeborn sons and daughters, slaves neither to privilege nor to unfair circumstance.

This counter-cultural message about freedom must not be softened. Yet how does one recover a word synonymous with the permission (and even encouragement) to be as selfish as one wants, especially in regard to the right to acquire as many material resources as one's power (personal, national, corporate) enables? How do we retool our lives lived long in a shadow world of quasi-freedom?

In the act of reading Shasta and Aravis's story, I participate imaginatively in the journey of wounded but beloved children tempted to live perpetually in Calormen habits, even while fleeing its geographic borders. While I read, I am changed. Of course, far too soon the last chapter of the text (whether Johannine, Pauline, or Narnian) ends. The tasks, even more than before, *await us*. What if we turn again to our routines and duties *indwelt* by these narratives? If so, then we may return to the tasks (at times great, but mostly small) to which we have been chosen and called to care about—return to them not to control, but to be available, eager to serve. No longer slaves, we are sons and daughters, heirs of the Father after whom every family on earth has its true identity.

4

Till We Have Christians:
A Myth of Christendom Retold (Matt 20)

Then the mother of the sons of Zebedee came to him, with her
sons, and kneeling before him she asked him for something . . .
Command that these two sons of mine may sit, one at your right
hand and one at your left, in your kingdom. You do not know
what you are asking . . . are you able to drink the cup that I am to
drink? . . . and when the ten heard it, they were indignant at the
two brothers. But Jesus called them to him and said, You know
that the rulers of the Gentiles lord it over them, and their great
men exercise authority over them. It shall not be so among you;
but whoever would be great among you must be your servant and
whoever would be first among you must be your slave; even as the
Son of man came not to be served but to serve, and to give his life
as a ransom for many (Matt 20:20–28).

L EWIS NEVER READ THE daily paper, never watched television, and
rarely went to the movies. In his inaugural lecture as the Professor of
Medieval and Renaissance Literature at Cambridge, he likened himself to
a dinosaur, a useful specimen more at home in the old Western order than
the modern. Yet forty years after his death, all of his Christian writings are
still in print. A one hundred fifty million dollar movie of *The Lion, The
Witch, and the Wardrobe* was released by Walt Disney just a few years ago.
How can it be that someone so perennially popular as Lewis was famous
for his resistance to modernity?[1] In this chapter I want to suggest that near
the core of Lewis's resistance to modernity was an indwelt experience of
medieval Christendom's hierarchical worldview, *but in an inverted way.*
In other words, Lewis inverts the medieval hierarchical universe (which
he loved) by the inversion of power into service. His indwelt experience

1. Lewis, *Selected Literary Essays*, 13.

of this inversion stirs our jaded imaginations still. This central gospel reality that gripped Lewis points toward an intentional missionary strategy that not only will provide a robust resistance to the thinness of modernity but also open a way beyond resisting modernity to constructing a positive post-Christendom and postmodern engagement with the world.

THE INVERSION OF POWER INTO SERVICE

In his most theologically ambitious work, *Miracles*, Lewis describes the coming of God in Christ as a descent and re-ascent

> like a strong man stooping lower and lower to get himself underneath some great, complicated burden or a diver in search of a lost pearl who first reduces himself to nakedness . . . then gone with a splash, vanished, rushing down through green and warm water into black and cold water, down through increasing pressure into the death-like region of ooze and slime and old decay; then up again, back to color and light, his lungs almost bursting, till suddenly he breaks surface again, holding in his hand the dripping precious thing that he went down to recover.[2]

Christ's resurrection eternally validates the way of using power for service. We are shown no other way by which sinners are redeemed and severed relations are restored, not only with God, but ecologically speaking, with the universe.

For Lewis, this pattern is not a mere novelty of the redemptive economy. In heaven itself, the trinity eternally gives and receives love in a mutual co-inherence, which is the interior grammar of God's being as Father, Son, and Holy Spirit. We glimpse this cosmic pattern in *Perelandra*, as the eldila participate in the Great Dance of humbly giving and in turn receiving honor and love.[3] In a heavenly suburb portrayed in *The Great Divorce*, Lewis has many re-orienting experiences when he steps off the bus from hell. In one of these he mistakes a humble Londoner (Sarah Smith from Golders Green) for the Virgin Mary. How did he commit such a blunder? Because in heaven one sees no longer through a glass darkly. When he looked upon Sarah Smith, she was clothed in her deeds of self-forgetful love, a garment she wore daily in a humble, working-class neighborhood of London.[4] But in heaven our eyes behold the splendor of these clothes.

2. Lewis, *Miracles*, 135.

3. Lewis, *Perelandra*, 214.

4. Lewis, *The Great Divorce*, 98.

The glory nearly overwhelms him. At the very beginning of Narnia, in *The Magician's Nephew*, Lewis offers a heaven's eye view of true British royalty when Aslan selects Frank, a working-class cab driver, and his wife, Helen, to be Narnia's founding king and queen. Something about their style and manner on earth uniquely qualified them for Narnia's highest office.

Whenever Jesus's kingdom touches earth, the pattern recurs. In *The Four Loves*, Lewis writes practical counsel on family love. He describes how the inversion of dominance into service epitomizes the healing of domestic life, whether through courtesy around the family dinner table or within the intimacies of husband and wife relations. The principle behind both domestic and public courtesy is the same: "That no one give any kind of preference to himself." Whereas in public a ritual or formal rules of good behavior allow civil life to function more or less smoothly, at home things must go deeper. "At home you must have the reality which that ritual represented, or else the deafening triumphs of the greatest egoist present. You must really give no kind of preference to yourself; at a party it is enough to conceal the preference . . .Those who leave their manners behind them when they come home from the dance or the sherry party have no real courtesy even there. They were merely aping those who had."[5]

In 1951 there occurred an invitation for a special kind of public preferment when Lewis was offered a CBE in the Conservative government's honor's list. In his letter of refusal to the prime minister's secretary, Lewis said he did not wish to give his critics evidence that his writings were simply "covert anti-Leftist propaganda," which the receiving of kudos from a Tory government might imply.[6]

Lewis's refusal reveals a missionary's strategy: to resist the yoking of "mere Christianity" with establishment patronage and/or British nationalism. The alternative approach is well depicted in his study of Milton's *Paradise Lost*. There Lewis portrays Lucifer as the epitome of aspira-

---

5. Lewis, *The Four Loves*, 43–4. On marriage, see 98.

6. "I feel greatly obliged to the Prime Minister, and so far as my personal feelings are concerned this honour would be highly agreeable. There are always however knaves who say, and fools who believe, that my religious writings are all covert anti-Leftist propaganda, and my appearance in the Honours List would of course strengthen their hands. It is therefore better that I should not appear there. I am sure the Prime Minister will understand my reason, and that my gratitude is and will be none the less cordial." 3 December, 1951, to the prime minister's secretary, in reply to the offer of a Commander of the British Empire, *Letters of C. S. Lewis*, edited by W. H. Lewis, 235.

tion for privilege and honors.[7] The chapter on "The Great Sin" in *Mere Christianity* identifies the longing for preferment and power over others as the utter core of how pride corrupts heaven and earth.[8] If we return to *Perelandra*, we see how, rather than empty himself in loving service, the malevolent Weston traces his evolution to higher consciousness as the steady abandonment of the notion of self-sacrifice in favor of what he terms "utility," by which he *unites and identifies* the serving of himself *with* serving the purpose of the universe. What was the training ground for this egoistic absorption of the universe's purpose into his own self-aggrandizement? Lewis describes something uncomfortably familiar: "I wanted scholarships, an income, and that generally recognized position in the world without which a man has no leverage."[9]

But in Lewis's baptized universe, the highest never stands without the lowest. Even the animal world shall taste the transformation of its self-preferential, jungle ways through descent into service. Indeed, there can be anticipations even now. George Sayers recalls a walk with Lewis past a field of pigs. On the other side of the fence there was a sow who seemed to approach them hoping for a snack. "Jack rubbed her back with a stick, saying 'I'm afraid I've no food for you, but perhaps like most human beings you will enjoy having your back scratched.' Just then a younger or at least smaller pig came over with a bundle of hay it had carried from the far part of the field. It laid the hay down in front of the sow and stood a few feet away watching her eat. Jack was astonished. 'George, this animal has been transformed. It has been touched by grace and raised to a higher level. What unselfishness! It must be hungry too! George, we are witnessing something extraordinary. We are witnessing the birth of the first *pog*.' Then he addressed the *pog* in courtly language, welcoming him into 'this corrupt world and beseeching such blessing as you are able to give.' Strangely, the *pog* looked at us and grunted apparently in answer. Then Jack said, 'George, let us move on, before the spell is broken, or lest we offend his honour by our vulgar staring.'"[10]

7. Lewis, *A Preface to Paradise Lost*, 94–103.

8. Lewis, "The Great Sin," 111.

9. Lewis, *Perelandra*, 89.

10. Saver, *Jack*, 203.

A MISSIONAL CONVERSATION: BREAKING
THE POWER-AS-DOMINANCE ENCHANTMENT

In the kingdom Jesus proclaimed, he taught his disciples to pray *lead us not into temptation, but deliver us from evil.* If Jesus used power to descend into service, how do we break the enchantment that whispers (or shouts) that power is for self-interest, control, and superiority? Here I raise this question in conversation with the world church in order to describe both a way of converting power *and* of being empowered for service. Let us begin with Kwame Bediako, the Ghanaian theologian, who saw in African primal religion a challenge to express Christianity not simply in conceptual systems but in the idiom of a lived encounter with other powers and principalities in everyday life.[11] Of course, the language of "power encounter" can be easily hijacked along a Zebedee path, as noted in Paul Gifford's citation of growing Pentecostal churches in Ghana, which seem to perpetuate the pathologies that surround them by "insisting upon success, wealth and status."[12] Another cross-cultural voice, Paul Freston, has described the failure of Christian imagination to revisit the meaning of empowerment for daily living when the official organs of the Assembly of God church in Brazil declare that because their movement is led by the Holy Spirit, it is consequently "immune to the natural factors which condition human societies." Such rhetoric leads the church to "stress heroism and exceptional events, neglecting the normal and mundane."[13]

By contrast, Bediako writes of a theology of encounter that is not so much about the extraordinary as the everyday, where the miraculous occurs when the church is open to a unique kind of divine encounter, "a sign of divine vulnerability, redemptive suffering, and reconciling love not as abstract notions but as concrete events and deeds in a human life."[14]

---

11. Bediako, *Jesus and the Gospel in Africa*, 95–6.

12. See the review by Ogbu Kalu of Gifford, *Pentecostalism in a Globalising, African Economy*, in *IBMR*, 160.

13. Freston, "Contours of Latin American Pentecostalism," 224. On a more positive note, Freston reports that one reason for the great popularity of Pentecostalism amongst women is that, though it appears to reinforce conservative stereotypes of gender role inequality, it powerfully resocializes men away from the destructive patterns of machismo. When Christ becomes the new model of leadership for men, they reinvest their time and money in the family and the children (258).

14. Bediako, *Jesus and the Gospel in Africa*, 42.

Deeds of love make a felt connection with real life. Without them others will not recognize Jesus as Lord. Though Bediako has in mind an issue from his own country, this is not confined to Ghana, for it lies at the core of Christian-Muslim differences in the actual living of one's life. Citing John Taylor and Kenneth Cragg, Bediako contrasts the way of Jesus, to die on the cross in suffering love for his enemies, and the way of Mohammed, to take up the sword and defeat his enemies in defense of the truth.[15] The task of Christian theology in a missionary setting is to provide conditions that translate these ideas about God's fundamental nature into more than ideas, but fundamentally into a way to live. The missional question we must ask therefore is do Christians who are connected to Jesus and his story enable or empower our near and distant neighbors, *including our enemies,* to make a personal decision to respond?

This missional conversation is deepened by Lesslie Newbigin's suggestion that Islam, like Marxism, identifies ultimate truth with actual political power. He argues that, by contrast, the union of truth with power for Christians "lies beyond death" and in that sense Christianity has an essentially otherworldly component, that is, one in which heaven cannot simply be absorbed by earth. But this doesn't mean the church should allow faith to be privatized. He insists the truth claims of the gospel are intended to challenge the public life of the world as much as the private. Part of a proper gospel challenge entails the exploration of the relationship between God's justification of sinners by grace and human justice. Hence the missional imperative of the church increases the tension between the entire human story and the story of Jesus. In each generation and culture, the church bears witness to the gospel as foretaste, sign, and instrument of God's kingdom "on earth as in heaven." While never a theocracy in an Islamic sense, every church ought to naturally (gracefully) offer up parables that engender a kind of human behavior whereby human agents operate for the common good.[16]

So how can an Oxford don who wrote largely in the fourth and fifth decades of the last century help us form a post-Christendom, postmodern missional strategy for today? I suggest he has done so by building a bridge from a modernist apologetic (defending Christianity as a series of ideas) to a postmodern apologetic, that is, expressing a Christianity that engages the world with the gospel through the living of a missional life. At

15. Ibid., 45.

16. Newbigin, *A Word in Season,* 197.

the core of Lewis's resistance to modernity was a refusal to accommodate Christian doctrine for fear of offending contemporary plausibility structures. That is why he considered Rudolf Bultmann's de-mythologization campaign closer to *mere* syncretism than mere Christianity. No, says Lewis, the miraculous element is part and parcel of the biblical witness to Jesus as Lord, Redeemer of earth as well as heaven, history as well as story, fact as well as myth. But even more important for our topic, Lewis understood that *no system of ideas* can reshape our world, either the outer world or our private one. No empowerment of the Church for witness is possible without a bold recovery, not a retirement, of biblical imagery and metaphor. In other words, Lewis sees metaphor and story as vessels of transformation in which doctrines believed by the head are felt in the heart and begin to alter and redeem the desires of the belly. "Without the aid of trained emotions the intellect is powerless against the animal organism."[17] For his readers, Lewis breaks the Zebedee enchantment in regard to power by packing depth charges of metaphor and story to explode in our imaginations, to reconstruct our all too natural longings and desire for power as status for ourselves and dominance over others.

In other words, to break the spell of a power-for-dominance paradigm, we need more than sound theological ideas. We need a Puddleglum who will put his foot in the fire and let the smell of burned Marshwiggle fill the air and clear our heads of the dualisms that fancy an autonomous earth or supposes that Jesus's authority rules the heavens all right but has no power or relevance on earth, never has, never will. Thrum. Thrum. Thrum. Does this mean that the millions who viewed the Disney movies of *Narnia* were suddenly disenchanted with the normal, self-serving fodder they are fed in our media-saturated West? Some perhaps, while for others perhaps the tiniest of mustard seeds was subversively planted.

Frankly, releasing people from the dominant power for self-aggrandizement enchantment, which is the daily bread of our culture, could use some reinforcement from spheres beyond the cinema. I am aware that Christian preaching has a well-deserved reputation for soporific qualities, but for the pulpit to thump once again and alert us to the Zebedee longings for power might help put an end to childish ways. Wherever the prophetic venue, long overdue are words to challenge the tendency of governance structures in education, politics, and church to form inner circles or inner rings that feed our sense of acquiring personal worth by the dominance over or exclusion of others.

17. Lewis, *The Abolition of Man*, 13.

As noted already, Bediako believed a genuine encounter between Christ and the meanings inherent in other religions only occurs in the vulnerability and suffering love manifest in Jesus's own method. That is why a mere intellectual debate between belief systems sidesteps the heart of the matter and can reduce Christian speech to just another power play. Required instead is participation in a *lived encounter*. I offer three suggestions from Lewis on how such enacted Zebedee encounters can arise in a postmodern world.

HOSPITALITY

In his favored genre, *Märchen* or fairy tale, Lewis found it irresistible not to welcome various pagan deities and their devotees into his world of Narnia. Some, like Tash, who suspiciously resembles mother Tiamat of Ancient Babylonian fame, is straightforwardly a nasty piece of work. Yet one of her followers, *Emeth* (Hebrew for faithful, true), is clearly worthy of a better god than Tash, as readers of *The Last Battle* discover. Elsewhere, there is the mischievous Bacchus, the Greek god of wine and ecstasy, who makes a joyful and frenetic guest appearance. Lewis's welcome of this mischievous deity includes a warning, well expressed by Susan's retrospective assessment to Lucy:

> "I wouldn't have felt safe with Bacchus and all his wild girls
>   if we'd met them without Aslan."
> "I should think not," said Lucy.[18]

Indeed, such a measured response is appropriate in any world, real or imagined, wherever one encounters Bacchus.

The plumb line that measures Bacchus or Tash is the lion who is the lamb. Lewis's created world welcomes such divine figures and energies, not as rivals detracting from the lion's reality, for to borrow Tolkien's phrase, they actually "assist in the effoliation and multiple enrichment" of the redeemed creation.[19] The logic of Lewis's hospitality raises questions for us: What is our favorite genre? Where do we do our best work and delight most deeply? How can we practice hospitality in these spaces, rather than hostility or avoidance?

18. Lewis, *Prince Caspian*, 138.
19. Tolkien, "On Fairy Stories," 73.

CHRISTIAN APOLOGETICS IN A NEW IDIOM

A lived missional encounter of a world church with a wounded world can do worse than begin with a newly *vulnerable* Christian apologetics—to be blunt, an apology. Perhaps, muses Lewis, a new book needs to be written about Christendom's past.

> If ever the book which I am not going to write is written it must be the full confession by Christendom of Christendom's specific contribution to the sum of human cruelty and treachery. Large areas of "the world" will not hear us till we have publicly disowned much of our past. Why should they? We have shouted the name of Christ and enacted the service of Moloch.[20]

These words suggest we need to read the history of Christendom as a tragedy whose own contradictions led both to its disruptions East and West (including the later Protestant revolt) and its eventual discarding (or syncretization) by the Enlightenment and modernity. But just as an "enlightened" reader of history might have supposed Christianity was coming to its deserved end, the Spirit blew where it willed and gospel seed germinated in surprising ways and places. There is no bigger surprise in the Protestant world than the modern missionary movement itself, springing from Zinzendorf and the Pietists on the continent and William Carey and others in Great Britain. To think this movement arose, as Karl Barth noted, not in the days of Christianity's cultural dominance but during its time of declining status in the Enlightenment testifies to the peculiar power of the gospel, which often appears in the context of our personal weakness.[21] As the Lord reminded Paul:

> My grace is sufficient for you, for power is made perfect in weakness. So I will boast all the more gladly of my weaknesses, so that the power of Christ may dwell in me (2 Cor 12:9–10).

Perpetually is Christendom—Byzantine, Roman, and Protestant—tempted to adorn itself as the city of God on earth. It dons the mantel of dominance, power, and conquest rather than reaches for the towel of loving service. Then, just when the church seems beyond remedy, along comes a counter-intuitive empowering of the church. It can even take the form of confession before the nations of our repeated failure to implement

---

20. Lewis, *The Four Loves*, 49.
21. Barth, *Church Dogmatics*, volume IV/3, part one, 20.

and live out of the gospel. Today apologetics as apology is being spoken in unexpected forms, including Christian teams from Youth with a Mission on pilgrimage in lands once crusaded through. It is there in the popular author Donald Miller's memoir of a postmodern confession booth at the highly secular (and Bacchanalian) Renn Faire at Reed College in Portland, Oregon.[22] At times the encounter that initiates the journey to conversion begins simply by uttering the words, "I am sorry."

A CRITIQUE OF THE AMERICAN AGENDA: "WE HAVE NO RIGHT TO HAPPINESS"

But words of confession without real change are smokescreens for manipulation. If an inversion of power truly emboldens us for service, has Lewis any suggestions for an economic translation of a gospel inversion of power in our world? Consider, as Tom Gettman of World Vision has said, that forty thousand people have died from terrorist acts in the past ten years. Meanwhile the same number die every day of preventable disease related to poverty. (Are we fighting the wrong terrorists?)[23] Though Lewis rarely ventured into questions regarding the economic implications of the gospel witness, he actually has several clear guidelines.

In our personal giving, "I am afraid the only safe rule is to give more than we can spare."[24] Walter Hooper records that Lewis regularly gave away two-thirds of his royalties.[25] For a child who grew up without a mother and with a father who worried constantly about money, this was not a pain-free behavior. As for macro economic issues, his essay on "Equality" (written in the midst of the Second World War and with a keen sensitivity to the Marxist dangers of a "flat equality") is quite clear: "Legal and economic equality are absolutely necessary remedies for the Fall, and protection against cruelty. . . We Britons should rejoice that we have contrived to reach much legal democracy (*we still need more of the economic*) . . ." (emphasis added).[26] Moreover, Lewis would have none of the dualisms that would permit selfishness as public policy and confine charity to the home. "It is our business . . . to follow in private or in public

---

22. Miller, *Blue Like Jazz*, 113–28.
23. Tom Gettman, public lecture, George Fox University, November 11, 2005.
24. Lewis, "Social Morality," 81.
25. Green and Hooper, *C.S. Lewis, A Biography*, 200.
26. Lewis, "Equality," 18, 20.

life, the law of love and temperance even when they seem to be suicidal, and not the law of competition and grab, even when they seem to be necessary to our survival."[27]

Christians in each nation cannot bear witness in an economically united "globalized" world unless we remind our governments (and they constantly need reminding) that continued international economic inequalities simply increase cruelty. If the Christian communion within each society would make this as clear as Lewis did, our apology might well be heard as genuine. That this may conflict with other economic agendas Christians should honestly acknowledge as part of our faithful witness.

The last article Lewis wrote before his death was published in the popular American magazine, *The Saturday Evening Post*. In it he sharply challenged how the "right to happiness" of our founders' vision could provide guidance for the future of humankind. To give unfettered "rights" to any desire, including the desire for monetary gain, is simply avarice. Yet such a right is regularly identified as basic to that most sacred of American words, "freedom." Such freedom fosters a society "in which not only each man but every impulse in each man claims *carte blanche*. And then, though our technological skill may help us survive a little longer, our civilization will have died at heart, and will—one dare not even add 'unfortunately'—be swept away."[28]

CONCLUSION: "RIGHTLY UNDERSTOOD, THERE ARE NO CHRISTIANS"[29]

I close this chapter by linking Karl Barth's unsettling diagnosis from 1918 as a response to G. K. Chesterton's question penned in 1910: "What's wrong with the world?"[30] At the beginning of the twentieth century, Chesterton said something to the effect that Christianity had not been tried and failed. It had been found difficult and not attempted. Writing in the wake of World War I, Barth wrestled to understand the tragedy of how the leading nations of Christendom had so energetically tried (with God on their side) to destroy one another. Surely the problem transcended a debate about whether Europe lacked a critical mass of individual believ-

---

27. Lewis, "On Living in an Atomic Age," 79.
28. Lewis, "We Have No Right to Happiness," 322.
29. Barth, *The Epistle to the Romans*, 321.
30. Chesterton, *What's Wrong with the World*.

ers. William Temple in 1914 suggested we should add a new clause to the Apostles' Creed: "I believe in the Holy Catholic Church and regret that it does not exist."[31] These honest questions and penitential responses did not, at the launch of the twentieth century, nor will they today, in the first decade of the twenty-first, deliver a devastating public relations blow to Christianity. Quite the contrary, if the Christian emblems worn by the kings and queens of Christendom past, and more recently by Christian presidents, prime ministers, and their chaplains, were and are largely ceremonial, the sooner we confess it, the better. Let us admit with candor that beneath the robes of official Christianity lays quite a lot of good old naked paganism.

If the open secret of Christianity is that "God so loved the world," then the ever-popular Sunday school refrain, "Jesus loves me, this I know" disguises the great Babylonian captivity of our (postmodern, post-Cold War) times. Of course "Jesus loves me" can be a joyful personalizing of the gospel famously declared in John 3:16. But it can also be symptomatic of a titanic self-aggrandizement, an ambiguous evangelical translation of Weston's mindset in *Perelandra*. What I am saying is that we habitually substitute *me* for the world. That is why the most serious global question for a missional church agenda today has become the inversion of Luther's question, "Where can *I* find a gracious God?" into "How can *the nations* (all of them) find a gracious God?"

So where does this leave us today, when pundits and philosophers of history describe variously as "the end of history," the "clash of civilizations," the decline of "the American Empire," and the postmodern entrails of modernity? Without controversy we can assert that the power-grasping agenda of the Zebedee brothers and their aspiring mother has cast a persistent shadow, amply contributing to what Tolkien has called the gospel's long defeat in history.[32] But as long as the Holy Spirit descends to brood upon the Church, to stir up among us the presence of Christ, hope will not be extinguished, though it will be accompanied (quite appropriately) by sighs and groans (Rom 8:23–25). For "the light shines in the darkness and the darkness has never mastered it" (1 John 1:5)—till we have Christians.

---

31. Quoted from Temple's 1914 book, *Christianity and War* in A. J. Hoover, *God, Germany and Britain in the Great War, A Study in Clerical Nationalism*, 126.

32. Tolkien, *Letters of J. R. R. Tolkien*, 255.

PART TWO

Reading the Bible as a Double Narrative

5

A Theology of Nature and of Grace for a Silent Planet
(Ps 19; Rom 1–2)

The heavens are telling the glory of God; and the firmament proclaims his handiwork. Day to day pours forth speech and night to night declares knowledge. There is no speech, nor are there words; their voice is not heard; yet their voice goes out through all the earth, and their words to the end of the world.

In the heavens he has set a tent for the sun, which comes out like a bridegroom from his wedding canopy, and like a strong man runs its course with joy. Its rising is from the end of the heavens, and its circuit to the end of them; and nothing is hid from its heat.

The law of the LORD is perfect, reviving the soul; the decrees of the LORD are sure, making wise the simple; the precepts of the LORD are right, rejoicing the heart; the commandment of the LORD is clear, enlightening the eyes; the fear of the LORD is pure, enduring forever; the ordinances of the LORD are true and righteous altogether. More to be desired are they than gold, even much fine gold; sweeter also than honey, and drippings of the honeycomb.

Moreover by them is your servant warned; in keeping them there is great reward. But who can detect their errors? Clear me from hidden faults. Keep back your servant also from the insolent; do not let them have dominion over me. Then I shall be blameless, and innocent of great transgression. Let the words of my mouth and the meditations of my heart be acceptable to you, O LORD, my rock and my redeemer (Ps 19).

Ever since the creation of the world his eternal power and divine nature, invisible though they are, have been understood and seen through the things he has made. So they are without excuse; for though they knew God, they did not honor him as God or give thanks to him, but they became futile in their thinking, and their senseless minds were darkened. Claiming to be wise they became fools; and they exchanged the glory of the immortal God for images resembling a mortal human being or birds or four-footed animals or reptiles . . . (Rom 1:20–23).

But as for you who bear the name of Jew and rely on the law: you take pride in your God; you know his will; taught by the law, you know what really matters; you are confident that you are a guide to the blind, a light to those in darkness, an instructor of the foolish, and a teacher of the immature, because you possess in the law the embodiment of knowledge and truth. You teach others, then; do you not teach yourself? You proclaim, 'Do not steal'; but are you yourself a thief? You say, 'Do not commit adultery; but are you an adulterer? You abominate false gods; but do you rob shrines? While you take pride in the law, you dishonor God by breaking it. As scripture says, 'Because of you the name of God is profaned among the Gentiles (Rom 2:17–24).

THE BEST AND THE WORST

FOR SHEER POETRY, LEWIS rates the nineteenth Psalm the best in the Psalter. He wants us to notice how its unforgettable descriptions are tied to cogent reasons. Thus the law is "Sweeter than honey," for it embodies the order of the divine mind.[1] The structure (six verses on nature, followed by five on the law, and concluding with four on personal prayer) progresses imaginatively, not by some logical order. Thus from nature (sky, sun, and heat, from which nothing is hid), the author jumps *intuitively* to law. "The law is undefiled, the law gives light, it is clean and everlasting. It is sweet. No one can improve on this description and nothing can more fully admit us to the old Jewish feeling about the law; luminous, severe, disinfectant, exultant."[2] Best of all, the writer is entirely free of self-righteousness, even requesting the law-giver to search out his hidden faults. "Search me, O God . . ." What should one do but try as much as possible to follow these guidelines? After all, God's laws have *Emeth* "truth," intrinsic validity, rock-bottom reality, rooted in the very nature of God, solid as the nature God has created.[3] Compared with the many false

1. Lewis, *Reflections on the Psalms*, 56.
2. Ibid., 57.
3. Ibid., 55.

paths of their neighbors, Israel's laws were a sure pathway. How can there be a better way to live?

Now comes the worst. The more Israel appreciated the law's grandeur and beauty compared to the pagan sea surrounding them, the more they were tempted to be smug. "We might then come to thank God that we are not as other men."[4] For Lewis, here is the greatest personal difficulty the Psalms raise. But he temporarily sets aside this worry in order to soak up the atmosphere of a mind enraptured by moral beauty, which is the spirit of this special Psalm.

We too might wish to linger a moment longer over the compelling connection between nature, law, and prayer felt by the Psalmist, partly because it led him to a closing crescendo of praise and partly because this linkage is virtually extinct in the human experience today. Many are the contemporary walks that take place under a powder blue sky without evoking thoughts about the ten commandments, the civil codes in Leviticus, or the complex subject of personal prayer. Nevertheless, for people of faith this psalm is often read as a kind of proof for the existence of God. It's the kind of logic we hear in evangelistic sermons where the preacher declares with utmost confidence, "I look in the microscope and I know there's got to be a God!" End of discussion.

As we've already seen, Lewis thought it quite important to distinguish between an imaginative connection and a logical one. We know from his correspondence with Bede Griffiths, his former pupil, that he was not a fan of Thomist natural theology, which argues by the laws of inference from observation of nature to nature's designer.[5] More publically, Lewis introduces his book on theodicy, *The Problem of Pain*, with the following lines from Blaise Pascal.

> I wonder at the hardihood with which such persons undertake to talk about God. In a treatise addressed to infidels they begin with a chapter proving the existence of God from the works of Nature . . . this only gives their readers ground for thinking that the proofs of our religion are very weak . . . It is a remarkable fact that no canonical writer has ever used Nature to prove God.[6]

4. Ibid., 57.

5. Lewis, *Letters of C. S. Lewis*, 242.

6. Quoted in Lewis, *The Problem of Pain*, 13. Apparently Griffiths challenged Pascal's exegesis of Scripture.

Pascal asserts that Scripture never uses nature to prove God; Lewis quotes him approvingly. Thus says Lewis, let us not use Psalm 19 as evidence in the case for proving God by inferences from nature. But *The Problem of Pain* goes further than simply expressing skepticism about this kind of natural theology. Lewis actually *reverses* the argument! He describes how for many years nature declared to him a god of grim Darwinian might-makes-right, where creatures survive by preying on one another, where the human creature, using reason and tool, exploits its powers to make war and crime at the center of the historical journey we euphemistically label the story of civilization, whose "progress" points not to a benevolent spirit, but to the very opposite. "Either there is no spirit behind the universe, or else a spirit indifferent to good and evil, or else an evil spirit."[7] Can you imagine a greater contrasting mood from the Psalmists' delight in gazing at the sky, the sun, the heat than the emotion of a pessimistic, young Lewis staring at the heavens, sensing, if any divinity, one indifferent to good or evil or darker still, a malevolent presence? Is the one mood simply right and the other utterly false? Or is it better to say the dark mood hints at the mystery of something glorious gone wrong, something, in fact, akin to what St. Paul describes in Romans regarding darkened minds and disobedience?

To guide us further into this shrouded area, I repeat a story told by the German theologian and pastor, Helmut Thielicke. He tells of an incident during the Second World War near Stuttgart when he was with some twenty boys from a school who that night were manning an anti-aircraft battery. As the local pastor in charge of catechism, he relates the following incident:

> They were anxious to have me come and give them religious instruction. . . So I walked out to visit them regularly and we sat down among the guns and talked about the "last things." But on this occasion they had called me for another reason. Their position had been hit by a low-level attack and the father of one of the boys, who happened to be visiting, was killed while his boy was manning the gun. The boy carried his dead father away in a wheeled stretcher. The youngsters—for that's all they were—crowded around me deeply shocked, almost like chicks around a hen. They were completely broken up and they looked to someone older for protection from a world whose dark enigma had sud-

7. Lewis, *The Problem of Pain*, 15.

denly leaped upon them for the first time. I spoke some words of comfort to them, though I myself felt utterly helpless.

But then the thing happened that accounts for my relating this incident at all. On my way home the moonlight lay upon the quiet valley, the white flowers of the trees shimmered in this soft light, and an unspeakable peace and stillness rested upon the landscape. The world was "like some quiet room, where wrapt in still soft gloom, we sleep away the daylight's sorrow."

I mention this, not be romantic or to gain a sentimental effect, but rather because for me this hour was a parable of the dark threshold which, the account of the Fall says, man has crossed. Before me lay the seemingly whole and healthy world of a springtime night. But in that moment *its very peace felt like a stab of pain*. For I knew that the peace of nature is delusive, and that I had just spoken, encompassed by a sea of blossoms, with boys whose eyes were filled with dread even though they bravely swallowed their tears.[8]

Thielicke's reflection upon the human condition reminds us of what Paul says in the early portion of Romans, as if a burden of heaviness hangs upon us and our world as a good thing spoiled. We are the Silent Planet, cut off yet connected by a painful memory, a place of extreme beauty alongside irreparable loss, "a place whose very peace at times feels like a stab of pain."

A Romans-eye view of this Psalm replies that the heavens sing a complex gloria, not a simple tune. Paul portrays a troubled awareness that amidst the marvel of creation, something has gone horrifically wrong. While Lewis never wrote a tightly reasoned exegesis of this text, he carefully describes the human dilemma, both in *Mere Christianity*, as well as in *The Problem of Pain*. The original context of *Mere Christianity* is worth remembering: Lewis is presenting the Christian faith to a nation in crisis, fighting for its survival against Nazi Germany. This book was his initial series of broadcast talks about Christianity over the BBC radio in August, 1941.[9] It was part morale booster, part interpreter of how Europe got into this desperate situation, and part map to help Britain find its way home. As we keep in mind this wartime situation, let us add a "supposal" connecting Lewis's exegesis in *Mere Christianity* to the German Pastor Thielicke's story. Together they clarify what happens when we read Psalm 19 alongside the crisis mood of Romans 1–2.

8. Thielicke, *How the World Began*, 121–2.

9. Green and Hooper, *C. S. Lewis, a Biography*, 202.

Suppose, amidst the numbness and dread of the German youth as they walk home that night with *Pfarrer* Thielicke, one of them imagines the bright, silent dawn gently rising not over Stuttgart, but over London, England. A London dawn would probably not be bright, but foggy, wet, and hazed with smoke and stench, but the point is the youth imagines what it must be like for British teenagers his own age walking this early dawn, perhaps with a parent or a padre after a night spent in the underground, the tube station, where many London families slept for safety as German bombers nightly pounded the city. But this evening, the German lad imagines his older brother flying a *Messerschmitt* on a raid over London. He envisions that he has made a direct hit on a power station where the father of the English family had been on firefighting duty that evening. That English father will never return home again because while he was working to put out the fire, the bombs released by his brother the Luftwaffe pilot made a direct hit on those fighting the flames.

Lewis portrays a world at war in which no one has clean hands. Even our sense of injury, our awareness of right and wrong, is tainted, slanted toward self-righteousness. We constantly blame others or excuse ourselves or conversely (and less commonly) blame ourselves and excuse others. As he puts it:

> Now I go back to what I said at the end of the first chapter, that there were two odd things about the human race. First, that they were haunted by the idea of a sort of behaviour they ought to practise, what you might call fair play, or decency, or morality or the Law of Nature. Second that they did not in fact do so . . .
>
> When I chose to get to my real subject in this roundabout way, I was not trying to play any kind of trick on you. I had a different reason. My reason was that Christianity simply does not make sense until you have faced the sort of facts I have been describing. Christianity tells people to repent and promises them forgiveness. It therefore has nothing (as far as I know) to say to people who do not know they have done anything to repent of and who do not feel that they need any forgiveness. It is after you have realized that there is a real Moral Law, and a Power behind the law, and that you have broken that law and put yourself wrong with that Power—it is after this, and not a moment sooner, that Christianity begins to talk. When you know you are sick, you will listen to the doctor. When you have realized that our position is nearly desperate you will begin to understand what the Christians are talking about. They offer an explanation of how we got into our present

state of both hating goodness and loving it . . . All I am doing is to ask people to face the facts—to understand the questions which Christianity claims to answer. And they are very terrifying facts. I wish it was possible to say something more agreeable. But I must say what I think true. Of course, I quite agree that the Christian religion is, in the long run, a thing of unspeakable comfort. But it does not begin in comfort; it begins in the dismay I have been describing and it is no use at all trying to go on to that comfort without first going through that dismay.[10]

Please note the *universality* of this dismay. Religion is famous for being tribal. It's us against them; our gods versus theirs. Not so Paul. He says the gospel tells of a broken world not just for his people, the Jews, on account of the bad behavior of Romans, Samaritans, and Idumeans. Of course, before his Damascus road, Paul was immersed in his exclusionary identity as a Hebrew of Hebrews, proudly sensitive of his victimhood and superiority from the Romans and other Gentile oppressors. But the gospel had shaken him to the core. It's not just Gentiles who are causing the problems in the world, and if only the Messiah would drive the Romans from Jewish territory (and might as well drive out the other races as well, Samaritans for starters), all would be well. No, says Paul, all of us, Jews *and* Gentiles, Gentiles *and* Jews, are without excuse *together*. *"Therefore you have no excuse O man, whoever you are . . ."* (Rom 2:1).

Lewis is certainly right about this severe diagnosis not beginning with comfort. But it lays the foundation for a new world as well as a new kind of community, where Jews and Greeks sit down together (alongside slaves and free, males and females, we may add), where the walls of separation (Ephesians) and blaming of the other *have been torn down*. Paul says that Gentiles are without excuse in their wrong conduct *and* so are Jews. It's a wasted effort to try to weigh who is more at fault. Moreover, the good news announces that a new community has now been launched to shine forth a new message into the old, dark world, which consists of all nationalities, united in a shared guilt and a shared hope that their moral and spiritual failure no longer has the last word. Their sin shall no longer imprison them in the endless cycle of aggressive incident, blame, and vengeance. The resurrection of the crucified Christ announces that a new world has broken into and turned upside down the old one of hatred, blame, and revenge. At the church's birth at Pentecost, the new world was

10. Lewis, "We Have Cause to Be Uneasy," 38–9.

demonstrably seen and heard to mercifully unite all tribes and nations. The initial sign of this new world was the outburst in multiple tongues as the good news was now shared by all nations. Rarely noted is the further miracle that comes next—the sharing of economic goods, thus enacting a parable of Jubilee hope.

Let us return to the supposal about the German youth that joins together a witness to the Creator's glory (Ps 19) with human dishonor and confusion (Rom 1–2): should the grieving youth perceive that the crisis of evil is no longer confined to the night skies over Stuttgart but includes the terror over London, his world shall change forever. The fault line of sin doesn't just run along enemy territory. Paul is wide awake to a guilty awareness of right and wrong, of how we make excuses for ourselves. And he insists we must confront the evil within us and our community as well as point the finger outward. This new grief-filled lens forms a new complex view of the dawn of every day.

During the summer of 2006 I first meditated on Thielicke's story when yet another convulsion of violence broke out in the Middle East, this time between Israel and Lebanon. I thought of the sons, daughters, and mothers walking home in silence both in Lebanese villages and in Northern Israeli cities like Haifa and the villages of Galilee. The nightly television news showed families pushing stretchers, families shattered irreparably by bombs. Thankfully, Lebanon and Israel arranged a ceasefire eventually. But as I write, the ongoing struggle in the region only increases week by week, month by month. And now my mind jumps back to Paul writing to an insignificant little group of Christians in Rome, meeting together in the center of empire. They have come together from a competitive mix of ethnic loyalties, which in the ancient world were fiercely tribal. It is not hard to imagine them discussing Paul's words about the *shared moral crisis* of Jews and Gentiles. I hear some of the Jews in Rome saying, "Paul, your good news may well be a valid insight, but please where is your *deepest* loyalty? Are you saying there's no basic difference between *us, your own people,* and the Gentiles? After all these centuries of divine history and your training under Gamaliel, is this the lesson you would teach us?" Next I hear some of the Gentiles, reading Paul's letter, wondering how a Pharisee-trained, law-embedded Saul/Paul can't but prefer his own nation's customs, rituals, and regulations. They are a little suspicious of his well-known patience and pleading with his own people, all this sympathy with Jewish history and custom. Indeed, there are rumors Paul has had Timothy circumcised just to please them! "Whose side are you really on, Paul?" Finally, I return to the present and recent past, and the debates/discussions I have had with friends (or former friends) at work, church, and home about who in our current crisis (here you can insert the one of the past year or month or week) is *really* to blame, who *really* started things, and where as God's people our true loyalties should lie.

Can you be *for* as well as *against* someone at the same time? Can you be for a nation and against its methods? Can you love sinners and hate sin? The gospel makes the claim to be for the world and against the world. St. Augustine in the fifth century contrasted the city of God and the city of man. He claimed they co-exist in history. The former city is motivated by service, love, and justice, the latter by domination, power, and conquest. He said the church's task was to bear witness to the city of God in every earthly city. That is the loyal opposition of the church in every city in which she finds herself. *For* the world, *against* the world, implementing Christ's strategy, not of an eye for an eye and a tooth for a tooth, not retaliation but intervention. Thus Saul of Tarsus mutates from a religious man of violence into an apostle of faith working through love.

TEMPORARY CONCLUSION:
WHAT DO THE HEAVENS DECLARE TODAY?

Today it is not possible to gaze into the heavens and simply see God's glory with the innocence of the ancient Hebrew poet. This is one of the primary lessons culled from Lewis's reading of Psalm 19. A Christian reader can no more read an Old Testament text *innocently* apart from cross and empty tomb than can we gaze at the heavens and read off the content of theology apart from Jesus's crucifixion in human history. Indeed, history as a place of disobedience and tragedy has grown increasingly violent since Rome's turn at empire. For too many villages and cities around the globe, the quiet silences of dawn are far too often a temporary, foreboding lull in the fighting, accompanied by the silence of muffled grief. In this awareness, Lewis concludes his reading of Psalm 19:

> All Christians know something the Jews did not know about what it "cost to redeem their souls." Our life as Christians begins by being baptized into a death; our most joyous festivals begin with, and centre upon, the broken body and the shed blood. There is thus a tragic depth in our worship which Judaism lacked. Our joy has

to be the sort of joy which can coexist with that; there is for us a spiritual counterpoint where they had simple melody.[11]

Beyond the usual tribe versus tribe, empire versus empire struggles, our contemporary star gazing lacks innocence because since the Psalm was composed, the One who created the heavens has himself suffered and been crucified, and it is only when this cross-shaped silhouette connects heaven and earth that we see God's glory in our far from innocent world.

DOES THE LAW STILL REVIVE THE SOUL?

Moreover, today when we meditate upon God's law, the result is not simply sweet but bittersweet, for a light shines upon *my* unclean hands, not just my adversary's. Revive the soul? It's more like being jolted awake by facts I am not eager to know. Listen again to Lewis's closing words from book 1 of *Mere Christianity*, from which I have framed our reading of Romans 1 and 2:

> I wish it was possible to say something more agreeable. But I must say what I think true. Of course, I quite agree that the Christian religion is, in the long run, a thing of unspeakable comfort. But it does not begin in comfort; it begins in the dismay I have been describing and it is no use at all trying to go on to that comfort without first going through that dismay.[12]

Given this uncomfortable way of reading the text, the final verse of Psalm 19 stands even *more* relevant than on the day first written: "But who can detect his own failings? Cleanse me of my hidden failings. Hold back your servant from willful sins lest they get the better of me."

A final incident from another summer of Middle East violence must be mentioned here. In Northern Israel, Pastor Elias Chacour runs a school in northern Galilee for both Muslims and Christians. It has regular visits and field trips back and forth with Jewish schools also. When the village and the school were caught in the midst of the summer of fighting, at the moment his village was surrounded by armies from both sides, he wrote these words: "We find ourselves between the fires of hatred on both sides both seeking to destroy the other." However he ends his letter with words of hope: "Be assured bombs shall stop, jet fighters shall be crippled.

11. Lewis, *Reflections on the Psalms*, 48.
12. Lewis, "We Have Cause to Be Uneasy," 39.

Children shall be able to play once again on the streets of our village; they shall go to school to learn that *together and only together they are stronger than any storm.* Yours sincerely, with tears and hope, Father Elias."[13]

With tears and hope. This aptly describe the lenses through which Paul now knows God in the strange new world the gospel has taught him to indwell. Though "meanwhile the cross comes before the crown and tomorrow is a Monday morning,"[14] in our labor *for* the world *against* the world, we don't lose hope. Though for the time being, hope joins with the labor pains of a new creation waiting to be born.

13. From Chacour, "Summer 2006.".
14. Lewis, "The Weight of Glory," 110.

6

Of Inner Rings and Rivals:
Rehabilitating the Doctrine of Election
(Gen 27; Rom 9–11)

Isaac finished blessing Jacob, who had scarcely left his father's presence when his brother Esau came in from hunting. He too prepared a savory dish and brought it to his father. He said, "Come, father, eat some of the game I have for you, and then give me your blessing." Who are you? His father Isaac asked him. "I am Esau, your elder son." he replied. Then Isaac, greatly agitated, said, "Then who was it that hunted game and brought it to me? I ate it just before you came in, and I blessed him, and the blessing will stand." When Esau heard this, he lamented loudly and bitterly. "Father, bless me too," he begged. But Isaac said, "Your brother came full of deceit and took your blessing" (Gen 27:30–35).

Even before they had been born or had done anything good or bad (so that God's purpose of election might continue, not by works but by his call) she [Rebekah] was told, "The elder shall serve the younger." As it is written, "I have loved Jacob but Esau have I hated." What then are we to say? Is there injustice on God's part? By no means! For he says to Moses, I will have mercy on whom I have mercy, and I will have compassion on whom I have compassion." So it depends not on human will or exertion, but on God who shows mercy (Rom 9:11–16).

W HEN I WAS A student in Aberdeen, Scotland, Professor James Torrance told a story of a confrontation between a young Scottish minister and one of his elders up in the Highlands, in an enclave of the severest school of High Calvinism: God loves the elect and hates the reprobate! The elder was alarmed about the tone of the sermons he'd been hearing from the young preacher. One day he came unannounced to the pastor's study and put his question quite directly to the young minister: "Do you believe that God hates sinners?" Taken aback, the minister said, "No! I believe God loves sinners!" The elder replied, "Then you're not true to the Bible. Jacob have I loved, but Esau have I hated, Romans 9:13." The minister thought for a moment and then replied, "Now let me put a question to you: do you hate your parents?" The elder was shocked at such a question and answered, "Certainly not! I love my parents." The minister replied, "Then you're not truly a disciple. Because Jesus said unless you hate your father and mother, you cannot be my disciple, Luke 14:26." Thus ended another irenic conversation between an elder and minister in Scotland.

How does the Bible use this word "hate"? Lewis suggests that Jesus (and Paul) use the word in a *relative* or *comparative* way, not an absolute way.[1] Jesus said you can't serve two masters; God and God's kingdom must come first, then parents, family, tribe, nation, all other loyalties— good and proper in their place not in God's—may rightly follow. As Lewis constantly reminds us throughout *The Four Loves*, if we turn this around, if we put career or family or ethnicity or national loyalty on the same level with God, that is idolatry. It puts second things first. When we thus exalt the creature in the place designed for the Creator, we corrupt everything. We become nepotists and warmongers. We may proudly declare our loyalty to our family, our ethnic/religious group, our gender, our nation, but when we put them in the place that belongs to God alone, we have violated the first commandment, "You shall have no other gods before me." That is the challenge that biblical monotheism everywhere addresses to our natural loves and identities.

The elder in Professor Torrance's story was in danger of a very serious misreading of the text. In an effort to honor God's authority, he read "hatred" not in a *relative* way, but in an *absolute* way—that there is in God an utter rejection and abandonment of (some) sinners, that God has an equal and as absolute an attitude of hate for some as love for others, as if fundamentally God is as hateful as loving.[2]

---

1. Lewis, *The Four Loves*, 171.

2. There are numerous places where Lewis makes his views clear. Cf. *Reflections on the Psalms*: "Such a view in effect makes God a mere arbitrary tyrant. It would be better and less irreligious to believe in no God and to have no ethics than to have such an ethics and such a theology as this" (54). Cf. also *English Literature in the Sixteenth Century*, 33–4, where Lewis sharply contrasts the development of the doctrine of Predestination

Where does this notion of an *absolute* hatred come from? Why would the Scottish elder attribute this darkest of passions to God? If we could understand these motivations, we would be a long way to correcting one of the great wrong turns in the history of Christian theology. The minister's rejoinder—that such logic would require we hate our parents—reveals the fallacy in treating this word in an absolute sense. That we are absolutely to hate our parents sounds forth as sheer offensive nonsense. Yet why has such nonsense often been attributed to God?

One of Lewis's longstanding existential concerns was the significance of rivalry and competition. One thinks of the dysfunctional, quarrelsome tone between Eustace and Jill at the start of *The Silver Chair*, which only makes their task far more dangerous and difficult. Earlier, in *The Lion, the Witch, and the Wardrobe*, Edmund's many grievances against his siblings make him vulnerable to the perverse charms of the White Witch. But for the resolute reactions of Mr. and Mrs. Beaver, his envy and jealousy would have destroyed them all. In *That Hideous Strength*, the young couple Mark and Jane Studdock are married and miserable as they strain their love through the filter of competing for dominance. Lewis's sobering essay, "The Inner Ring," explores the dark inversion of the deep longing to be accepted that "The Weight of Glory" enchantingly unveils. The tragic possibility exists in each of us; the secret longing to be enfolded in the glory of God's welcome can twist into the appetite to exclude and reject others.[3]

But his final novel, *Till We Have Faces*, tells a story that takes us to the heart of Paul's theology of the two brothers, Jacob and Esau. Lewis revisits the ancient Greek myth about Cupid and Psyche, and in his re-telling, gives Psyche an older sister, Orual (rhymes with cruel), and a father who is king of a small country. Psyche is very beautiful; Orual the elder, is very ugly—at least that's what her father abusively tells her. Eventually, Orual dons a veil—a cover up—rather than have her face despised any longer. But nothing can hide Psyche's beauty or her kindness. It makes her the object of fascination in the villages and in the court. When a harvest drought threatens the kingdom, Psyche is named, *chosen* by the priest, as the scapegoat, the only acceptable sacrifice to their god Ungit, so that the people may prosper again and the rains return. Initially distraught, her father agrees, for he prizes his kingship more than his lovely daughter

---

with the early Protestant experience of conversion.

3. Lewis, "The Weight of Glory," 94–111 and "The Inner Ring," 28–40.

and submits to the priest. So it comes to pass that many weeks later after Psyche is removed from the village and left tied to the cliff for the gods to devour, grieving elder sister Orual journeys to pay respects to Psyche's remains where she was left to die. But to Orual's utter astonishment, she finds Psyche alive and happily married to the god who came to rescue her. There is one puzzling piece to this bliss: her god/husband won't let Psyche see his face. Orual is absolutely convinced that, despite Psyche's happiness and joy, she has been tricked by enchantment into marrying a monstrous brute.

Orual decides that her loving duty is to persuade Psyche to disobey her husband so that when he sleeps, she must light a torch and see his face. Though she thereby will disobey her husband, she will know the truth that she has really been deceived into marrying an ogre. So desperate is Orual to rescue Psyche from this situation that she plunges a knife in her own arm as a suicide threat—to be carried out unless Psyche agrees to look upon her husband's face that very night. Grief stricken, Psyche knows full well this will be the end of her happy, settled life. Nevertheless, for love of her older sister, she agrees to do Orual's bidding.

That evening as Orual waits across the stream, watching for Psyche's torch to shine out in the darkness to expose the ogre, she can't stop thinking about how Psyche looked at her. Though Psyche agreed to her demand, Orual feels "un-loved, even *hated*. 'How could she hate me, when my arm throbbed and burned with the wound I had given it for her love? Cruel Psyche, cruel Psyche,' I sobbed."[4]

Hated? Yes, Orual's triumph was a tormented one because even as Psyche obeyed her, Orual sensed she preferred her husband. For Orual, this amounted to hatred. The rest of the book tells how Orual comes to face the truth about her "love" for Psyche, how in fact Psyche had no more cruel enemy than her. Finally, as Orual approaches death, and her own facing of the gods at her day of judgment, something happens by which she sees the truth about her "love" for Psyche. It overwhelms her to face the truth that her "love" for Psyche had mostly to do with jealousy, power, competition, and domination. At the moment of exposure before the gods and herself, Orual looks down in a pool of water. In its reflection, wonder of wonders, she sees two pair of feet—her own and Psyche's—"one clothed, one naked, and both beautiful (if that mattered now), beautiful

---

4. Lewis, *Till We Have Faces*, 149.

beyond all imagining, yet not exactly the same." Then a great voice speaks: "You also are Psyche."[5]

I won't ruin the ending for those who haven't read it, as this is enough to glimpse Lewis's agenda. Lewis has taken the old myth of Psyche and Cupid and reframed it according to the haunting biblical story behind the myth. It is a tale of twisted love, which we are doomed to repeat, unless, like Orual, we are granted a vision that puts to death one kind of love and restores us to a different love altogether. Thus Lewis revisits the story of the two brothers, Jacob and Esau, this tragic story of rivalry and twisted love, that afflicts the entire family—the parents Rebekkah and Isaac as well as brother Jacob the deceiver, the supplanter, who conspires with his mother to deceive his father to snatch the blessing from brother Esau, whose weakness and folly cause him to lose his place of honor in the family, which now shall descend through Jacob, who becomes Israel.

Meanwhile, amidst this fratricidal rivalry between love and hate, where is God? The Old Testament narrator doesn't say much except that providence is mysteriously at work, and that hatred and revenge will not have the last word in the story. But in the New Testament, is it coincidental that the most famous story Jesus tells is also a story about two rival brothers? As the Pharisees and lawyers of Israel listen to Jesus, they sense this story has to do with Israel's identity, indeed Israel's competition with her rival nations. After all, Israel was God's chosen one. Jacob was given the name Israel, and the Pharisees took enormous pride in being the children of Israel.

But a radical change occurs when Jesus re-tells Israel's story: this time the Father does not keep to the margins. With a costly welcome, he runs to interrupt the younger brother's humiliating, disgraceful return. The Father also pleads with the oldest, walking out into the night toward the resentful elder sibling, entreating him to join the banquet and enjoy what has *always* been his. But in Jesus's retelling, *both sons* need the blessing of reconciliation with the Father and please note, *with one another*. Mercy reaches out both to the prodigal and the elder. Shall the elder brother join the banquet? To borrow an image from *Till We Have Faces*, will the elder look down in the pool of mercy at his feet and see not one, but two brothers, both beautiful (if that mattered now) beyond all imagining, yet not exactly the same?

5. Ibid., 169.

ANOTHER DISTURBING RIVALRY

As I wrestle with this parable and its implications, it seems that we in today's church often enact the role of an elder brother who has dutifully labored in the Lord's vineyard now for two millennia. And we have a rival that can come across as very threatening. I mean the world, with its tawdry assortment of lapsed believers, heretics, pagans, atheists, skeptics, and misguided followers of inferior creeds. I call the world our great rival because Scripture awkwardly insists that God has compassion for all those many sheep not properly of the fold. This may be possibly the most awkward fact about Christian faith—that Jesus has a deep, enduring connection to outsiders, to prodigals, lost sheep, even to the thief on the cross. It is summed up famously in that verse that we church folk can read with a certain reserve: "For God so loved the *world*." I suspect that deep down, most of us lifetime and long-time believers think that, technically speaking, once you slice and dice away the hyperbole, in fact it really means God loves the *church*.

Let me be frank. I have been in the church my entire life and this word "world" has frequently provoked in myself (and I daresay in others) resentment, sometimes even "hatred" of the absolute kind. As a life-long believer, I can't begin to describe how many times I have been frustrated with the world and fed up with all the attention it gets. To put it more charitably, I am regularly disappointed that it is so resistant to the message of the gospel—certainly to the church as the official gospel messenger.

There is a wound here, undoubtedly. I sense an ache of longing whenever I recall the optimism I once felt that *my* generation might just succeed in winning the world for Christ! I can still see the *Time Magazine* cover story from my middle year in seminary with our new president, Jimmy Carter, smiling broadly on the cover with the caption that read: "The Year of the Evangelical." That year, 1977, was a very heady moment. Then I blink and more than thirty years have passed as the world keeps spiraling into increasing hateful rivalry. Closest to the tree is the fruit that has fallen in the Middle East itself, where the descendents of Isaac and Ishmael, Jacob and Esau (or their political leadership at least), seem as bent on mutual blame and recrimination as ever. Closer to home in the United States, our domestic rivalries, though usually less lethal, are ubiquitous, as the political left and political right, the rich and the poor, the politics of gender and sexual identity, all show no signs of lessening their tension and acrimony. What only exacerbates the pain is that these rivalries are never an equal fight. One side always seems preferred by the gods; the Esaus, elder brothers, and Oruals, ever resentful and revengeful, are never secure in winning the blessing they seek, ever resentful of an upstart favorite, yet hoping nevertheless to spoil the success should another be chosen. Consider our political world of rivals; which nation, great or small, seems eager to turn their swords into ploughshares? In Africa there are increasing reports of children abducted and turned into soldiers. Even soldiering itself, like all endeavors of large scale, has been lured into the economics of outsourcing. At the time I write, it is reported that there are more mercenary soldiers in Iraq than actual U. S. military.

Perhaps like me, you are weary of these kinds of headlines, weary of the politicians and heads of state eager to score at least verbal points should military victories not be easily forthcoming. Perhaps we are just tired of being tired, though often my own weariness has less than virtuous origins. Sometimes the elder brother who resides in me is jealous of the attention that sinners attract—sinners in the Middle East, sinners in Washington DC, sinners in our neighborhoods and families. As an older brother to my fellow farmhands and siblings, it seems as though we elder types have toiled with our time and talents in the Lord's vineyard these many years, and for what fruit? The world's media and movies have hardly noticed. They are endlessly fascinated with the glamour and the garishness of the world—the display of violence, lust, and greed show no sign of ceasing to dominate the headlines or the movies. Their self-assertive fashions even set the trend for church. Much of the time, the church attracts interest only when we wear some version of the same worldly garments— something flirtatious in our language or look, perhaps a powerful display of some sort, a pounding of the pulpit like a demagogue in training. Of course, should a church elder type mess up tragically, then of course the world pays rapt attention to every salacious detail.

My "elder brother's lament" can be stated like this: many times this prodigal world seems so much better at being the world than the church is at being church. Perhaps the church can't help being jealous of its success. Then, just to interrupt our complaint and add to our discomfort, we open our Bible and it reminds us that God loves this prodigal world and sent his only Son that it might not self-destruct. How can it possibly be true that the One Jesus called Father loves both, younger and elder, saint and sinner? How can I possibly live within this rivalry without becoming a partisan, caught up in competition and hatred of the one or the other?

Paul says there is only one possible way. To paraphrase Ephesians, he says one more beautiful than Psyche has been crowned with thorns and crucified to connect us both to God. This one has torn down the walls between all identity rivals. It has been accomplished not by fear, but by grace, not by coercion but by humble love, "Making peace by the blood of the cross" (Eph 2:13).

Whenever I read the Old Testament story of Israel, sometimes I identify with Esau begging for a blessing, having squandered through my weaknesses many privileges. At other times I am Jacob, having conspired with someone to snatch the family blessings (in as guilt-free way as possible, of course). "Please, Father, don't ask too many questions about how this stew came before you. Just bless me as your chosen." Part of me is a younger brother, having returned from the far country of self-seeking, now finally resigned to receive a portion of blessings alongside the elder types I have hitherto avoided. And always, I am well acquainted with the elder brother in me, who is distant and disapproving, skeptical of everyone's prayers and piety, including my own. But the text insists that the Father specially goes out into the field to invite the elder brother, comes and pleads with him. This entire assortment and conflicted assemblage of family members God summons with the words: "Come unto me you who are weary and heavy laden and I will give you rest" (Matt 11:29).

Suppose, as Clement of Alexandria once said, that Christ prefers each of us? To each of these rivalries, within us and without, in the church and in the world, between the church and the world, what if the gospel wants us to meet in communion? I have also supposed that the story of Psyche and Orual parallels the Jacob and Esau saga and like the saga we euphemistically call the story of civilization, the human story is a tale of competitive rivalry, a tale about the twist in love we are doomed to repeat in our theology and our politics, and in our neighborhoods and homes, unless we meet in a space where rivalry dies and is reborn as a new way of preferring and being preferred.

I am left with two questions. Where are the places of great rivalry in today's public world, especially those in which I am personally invested, that tempt me to do whatever it takes for my (our) share of the blessing? Where is the pool of water into which I can gaze and see not two rivals but two siblings, both beautiful? Where are the waters that transform ravaged spaces of competition into communion? There is a further question that broods beneath, the dark one with which this chapter began: What are the rivalries that urge me to refuse communion, to turn a relative preference into an absolute hate? If I could identify these, what would it cost to bring them close, hold them together and see "not one, but two rivals, both beautiful (if that mattered now) beyond all imagining"?

> Oh the depths of the riches and wisdom and knowledge of God!
> How unsearchable are his judgments and how inscrutable his ways
> (Rom 11:33)!

7

"Gawd, Ain't It Lovely?"
The Journey from Fear to Awe (Prov 1; Acts 4)

The fear of the Lord is the beginning of knowledge (Prov 1:7).

Now the whole group of those who believed was of one heart and soul, and no one claimed private ownership of any possessions, but everything they owned was held in common. With great power the apostles gave their testimony to the resurrection of the Lord Jesus, and great grace was upon them all. There was not a needy person among them, for as many as owned lands or houses sold them and brought the proceeds of what was sold. They laid it at the apostles' feet, and it was distributed to each as any had need . . . But a man named Ananias, with the consent of his wife Sapphira, sold a piece of property; with his wife's knowledge, he kept back some of the proceeds, and brought only a part and laid it at the apostles' feet. "Ananias," Peter asked, "why has Satan filled your heart to lie to the Holy Spirit and to keep back part of the proceeds of the land? While it remained unsold, did it not remain your own? And after it was sold, were not the proceeds at your disposal? How is it that you have contrived this deed in your heart? You did not lie to us, but to God!" Now when Ananias heard these words, he fell down and died. And great fear seized all who heard of it (Acts 4:32—5:5).

OUR STORY BEGINS IN the springtime of the early church when all things were held in common. Because of the resurrection of Jesus and a grace freely given, there was an incredible display of generosity one for another. This sharing was not some ideology being enforced on people, manipulating them. It was an eschatological fulfillment of the ancient words of Deuteronomy 15:4, "There should be no poor among you because God has given you his rich blessing." We might call this an economic proof of the resurrection. The logic goes something like this: The disciples have received such bounty that their joy compels them to generosity. Their sharing is not extracted; it's a natural response to grace. They are spreading a good infection. "Freely you have received. Freely give" (Matt 10:8). That's the beautiful logic lived here.

But the early church does not quite live happily ever after. Now comes a not-so-nice part of the story, just like today when not-so-nice things happen in our churches. Today, as in the text, both kinds of events take place. When believers gather and worship together, these are often the most beautiful moments of our week. We are together. It looks good. It feels good. The singing even sounds good (more or less). But that's never the whole story at church.

Along come Ananias and Sapphira. In many ways this is a very modern story in the way that it describes an egalitarian situation: the same thing happens to the woman as to the man! As they decide to sell their field, a marriage counselor might say they have a good marriage because they do it together. They even plan it together, down to the price. Unfortunately, they conspire to misrepresent their gift. While presenting it to the community as a total gift like Barnabus's field, which he gives completely away, they secretly keep a portion for themselves.

Peter gets the money but senses that something is wrong. He is very logical in his response. He says, "Why do you feel obliged to give? You are free! What is your problem?" He gets right to the heart of the matter when he says, "You lied to the Holy Spirit!" This is not really about finance and stewardship. This is about a loss of freedom in the church. But no love or faith is possible in the church without freedom.

This raises some questions: How do we live in the church? Are we free or are we under a lot of pressure? The first thing to understand about church is that it is a network of relationships. The first relationship is with God. But who can love God under pressure?[1] We are in the church because of forgiveness, not because of fear.

This episode shows what happens when people try to live in the church out of pressure and manipulation, instead of God's generosity. But what happens when we live in the church out of pressure? It creates a

---

1. See chapter 1, on Luther's dilemma and the turning of good news into should news.

psycho-somatic reaction.[2] Peter does not kill these people! If we want to be very critical, which is not the best way to view things, we might say that in the church there are sometimes cadavers. It's been said that the church is like a beautiful stream but that also has some dead dogs floating in it. Augustine puts it less crudely when he suggests that the church has wolves within it as well as sheep outside it.[3] And so the young people come and carry the dead away.

So what have we learned thus far? Sharing is something holy and brings new life. Sharing emerges from resurrected life. Not sharing and coercion bring death. We give because a sacred gift has been given to us first. As Brother Roger of Taizé often said, the secret of Christianity is God loves you first. We can't modify this, as if sometimes Christians can be formed into generous people by means of fear. God did not send Jesus out of fear. God does not fashion disciples out of fear.

But what about the famous words from Proverbs: "The fear of the Lord is the beginning of wisdom"? A first glance may suggest that the Old Testament is a fear-based religion and the New Testament is a religion of love. This line of thought soon takes us down Marcion's road, in which the Old Testament god is a cruel, fear-mongering deity defeated by Jesus. But the early church firmly rejected Marcionism by holding the two testaments (covenants) closely together, in the sense of promise and fulfillment. We need a better prescription for viewing these documents than Marcionite lenses.

A CLUE FROM HEBREW

In English we have two distinct words, fear and awe, with different connotations. A sense of awe in the presence of holiness, beauty, and goodness is a very different semantic environment from that which inspired Ananias and Sapphira to turn this sacred time of sharing into the church's first financial scandal. The Hebrew dictionary reveals that fear and awe translate the same Hebrew word and the translator must make a judgment which English word best fits the Hebrew context. So I suggest the following semantic lens: a sense of awe in the presence of God's beauty and love is the beginning of wisdom. Wisdom does not begin with the slave

2. I am indebted to Brother Wolfgang of Taizé, whose Bible study inspired much of this paragraph.

3. Augustine, *The City of God.*

mentality's fear of the master. Instead, deceit and trickery are the marks of trying to survive under pressure. Sometimes even in the early church people confuse these. That's what happened to Ananias and Sapphira.

CLUES FROM NARNIA

A sense of awe in the presence of God's holiness, beauty, and love—that's the beginning of wisdom. In *The Magician's Nephew*, Frank the cab driver along with a couple English school children, Jadis the witch, and a silly old wizard named Uncle Andrew all find themselves present in a dark space that seems like a vast nothingness but is actually the beginning of the new world, Narnia. As the Voice begins to sing the new world into being, Frank tells everyone to hush because the sound is so overwhelming he can hardly bear it. "'Gawd!' said the Cabby. 'Ain't it lovely?'" Suddenly the voice is joined by other voices, more than you can count, all up the scale in harmony, and just then instead of blackness overhead, blazing stars cover the sky.

> If you had seen and heard it, as Digory did, you would have felt quite certain that it was the stars themselves which were singing, and that it was the First Voice, the deep one, which had made them appear and made them sing. "Glory be!' said the Cabby. "I'd ha' been a better man all my life if I'd known there were things like this."[4]

That's the fear of the Lord that heals us, cleanses our imaginations, and purifies our heart's desires. But as noted already, we continually get things confused. Even as the cabby delights in this creation and allows it to work its natural cleansing response of repentance, another response is at work. Uncle Andrew hears the same Voice, but when he and the witch see the lion, their dislike of the Voice and the world that is forming takes in her very different reaction: "This is a terrible world. We must fly at once. Prepare the Magic." Uncle Andrew replies, "I quite agree with you, Madam . . . A most disagreeable place. Completely uncivilized. If only I were a younger man and had a gun."[5] This response reminds us of the moment when the children first heard the name Aslan in *The Lion, the Witch, and the Wardrobe*.

---

4. Lewis, *The Magician's Nephew*, 93–4.
5. Ibid., 96.

> At the name of Aslan each one of the children felt something jump
> in its inside. Edmund felt a sensation of mysterious horror. Peter
> felt suddenly brave and adventurous. Susan felt as if some delicious
> smell or a delightful strain of music had just floated by her. And
> Lucy got the feeling you have when you wake up in the morning
> and realize that it is the beginning of the holidays or the beginning
> of summer.[6]

Later on Mr. and Mrs. Beaver must help the children understand
the huge difference between Aslan's goodness and any idea of his being
"safe."

> "If there's anyone who can appear before Aslan without their knees
> knocking, they're either braver than most or else just silly."
> "Then he isn't safe?" said Lucy.
> "Safe?" said Mr. Beaver. "Don't you hear what Mrs. Beaver tells
> you? Who said anything about safe? 'Course he isn't safe. But he's
> good. He's the King, I tell you."[7]

We have learned from Lewis's sermon "Transposition" that we can't
prove from below there is a higher "awe" distinguishable from fear that
cleans us and makes us want to live better.[8] In terms of sheer physiological
effect, Uncle Andrew, the witch, Edmund, and Ananias and Sapphira may
have the same physiological flutters in the diaphragm as Frank the cabby,
Lucy, or Barnabus. Lewis also recalls how Samuel Pepys in love, Pepys
in hearing beautiful music, and Pepys in sickness had the same physical
sensation in his stomach.[9] Depending on the context, the reaction could
be highly desirable or highly disagreeable. We each interpret our physical
sensations according to the evolving interaction (and sometimes colli-
sion) between our inner world and the outer world.

Years ago I heard a famous preacher tell of an incident in his childhood when one summer he visited his grandparents in the country. One
day from behind the hedge between the properties, he looked out into
the next door field of the farmer and gazed at a big old farmer riding his
tractor. The boy longed to ride in this magnificent farm chariot, and his
longing drew him out a little ways beyond the hedge into the corner of

6. Lewis, *The Lion, the Witch, and the Wardrobe,* 65.

7. Ibid., 75.

8. Lewis, "Transposition," 77.

9. Ibid., 79.

the field where the man was tilling. Suddenly the man rose up from the tractor chair and started waving fiercely for him to get off his property. Embarrassed and frightened, the boy dashed home, even fearing now that the man might come over and tell his grandparents that he was guilty of trespassing. He spent a miserable Saturday night, hoping the man wouldn't come over to report his misdeed, hoping the man wouldn't be in church the next day. As inevitably as a Greek tragedy, when the congregation stood to leave the Sunday service, no matter how hard he tried to keep his distance from the angry man, the man reached out, gripped his shoulder, and pulled him aside. The boy looked up in anguish as the farmer spoke: "Young man, I saw you out on my field yesterday and I waved for you to come join me on the tractor, but you ran away! I'm riding again tomorrow morning, would you like to join me?" A smile broke out on the farmer's face. What had happened? Out of his fear, the boy had utterly misinterpreted the sign, transforming an invitation of welcome into an angry gesture of rejection. The farmer had actually been inviting the boy for a ride.

THE FEAR TACTIC

Now it must be acknowledged that over the centuries the church and her preachers have become accustomed to reach into their rhetorical tool kit to create an aura of mystery and fear as a vehicle for conversion. But this strategy reveals more about the anxiety in the preacher's soul than it does about the gospel. Lewis once noted how the preachers of a previous generation had exhausted their eloquence trying to induce fear of judgment in order to create a change of behavior.[10] But Lewis judged the effects of motivation through fear to be universally short term in their effects with many unforeseen negative side effects.

Of course, for short-term behavior modification, fear has its uses. The enslaved horse, Bree, finds through his fear of the chasing lion just the necessary strength to warn King Lune on time, despite all his years as a slave horse, which had habituated him to half-hearted efforts. As a parent I have used the short-term method at times when a reasoned discourse on bicycle safety would not have been adequate to warn that a car was rounding the corner *right now*.

10. Lewis, *Letters to Malcolm, Chiefly on Prayer*, 26.

I have used the short term for less worthy reasons also. So have governments and employers when it seems useful to keep citizens and employees easily controlled. Should a government wish to launch a war or terminate certain human rights, using the news and media to create a climate of fear against _____ (fill in the blank) seems to be often a political tool of choice to manipulate public opinion.

But according to Scripture, God seeks a quite different, holy kind of relationship, one in which fear (not awe), as a driving motivation, simply gets in the way. Lewis freely admits that he felt fear in the trenches of WWI, but he never "sank so low as to pray."[11]

The devil in the *Screwtape Letters*, puts it this way:

> To us a human is primarily food; our aim is the absorption of its will into ours, the increase of our own area of selfhood at its expense. But the obedience which the Enemy demands of men is quite a different thing. One must face the fact that all the talk about His love for men, and His service being perfect freedom, is not (as one would gladly believe) mere propaganda, but an appalling truth. He really does want to fill the universe with a lot of loathsome little replicas of Himself—creatures whose life, on its miniature scale, will be qualitatively like His own, not because He has absorbed them but because their wills freely conform to His. We want cattle that can finally become food; He wants servants who can finally become sons. We want to suck in, He wants to give out. We are empty and would be filled; He is full and flows over. Our war aim is a world in which Our Father Below has drawn all other beings into himself: the Enemy wants a world full of beings united to Him but still distinct.[12]

Paul writes: "You did not receive the spirit of slavery to fall back into fear, but you have received the spirit of sonship. When we cry, 'Abba, Father!' it is the Spirit himself bearing witness with our spirit that we are children of God, and if children, then heirs, heirs of God and fellow heirs with Christ" (Rom 8:15–16).

What is really going on in church? The coming of Jesus signals that God wants us to *share* in his holiness, not keep us separated. Sharing and generosity are at the very heart of the Holy Trinity. But in our fear, we turn God into an angry figure like the boy who turned the farmer into a man

11. Baker, "Near the Beginning," *Table*, 6.
12. Lewis, *The Screwtape Letters*, 45–6 (letter VIII).

of threats, furious at him for trespassing onto his property. Then church reacts like Ananias and Sapphira, or the little boy at the edge of the field, projecting our fear back into the gospel. We blind ourselves to what is really going on in the text and thus in our lives. The Scripture says when the Spirit of holiness came upon the early church, they were filled with the Spirit of generosity. We still need the Spirit's presence to sift our hearts and empty out the fear. When our fears cause us to misread the signs, the Spirit helps us to cry, "Abba, Father" as children, no longer slaves. "There is no fear in love. But perfect love casts out fear, because fear has to do with punishment. And the one who fears is not perfected in love" (1 John 4:16).

What is really going on in church? Upon leaving the holy sanctuary of God's presence, believers depart to homes or to work environments, either of which contain various levels of fear, perhaps toxic levels, where maybe not-so-nice things have happened and post-traumatic responses are common. Is it possible to return to these places in a new spirit, one based not on fear but based on the sharing of grace? In other words, is it possible to bring to such environments a sacred generosity and spirit of mercy that overcomes a spirit of judgment and rejection?

What is really going on in church? We are being schooled in a holiness that by transposition has shifted from separation to sharing. We are being swept up, like Frank the cabby, into an alarming generosity and creativity beyond anything we have imagined. How can this not evoke a new business-as-*unusual* connection with our neighboring world? I don't suggest this makes the world any less detached and avoidant or frightened and angry with God than before. There are no guarantees of visible success. Paul actually has the unsettling habit of mentioning suffering in the same breath as he does glory (Rom 8:17). We have been duly warned. But the Spirit who raised Jesus has not lifted our hearts in order to toss us aside into fear or manipulation. Rather, we are granted the Spirit of hospitality that indwells the triune sharing that Jesus names Father, Son, and Spirit.

What is really going on in church? Together we are learning how to share in the holiness that cries, "Abba Father."

8

Curses for Babylonians and Crumbs for Canaanites: A Hermeneutical Regress for Contemporary Pilgrims (Ps 137; Gen 22; Deut 7; Matt 15)

> I have written, too, as a member of the Church of England, but I have avoided controversial questions as much as possible. At one point I had to explain how I differed on a certain matter both from Roman Catholics and from Fundamentalists: I hope I shall not for this forfeit the goodwill or the prayers of either.[1]

RECEPTIVITY

THERE IS NO GREATER question for Bible interpretation than how Christians should interpret the Old Testament or Hebrew Scriptures, or as an implicit interpretative framework already would put it, "How should Christians interpret the Old Testament in light of the New?" One temptation for committed readers is to extract a divine word by chiseling away the humanity of the text or to change the metaphor, to filter out the human impurities in order to acquire pure doctrinal nuggets. But this purity approach to the text is as disastrous in studying the Bible generally as it is in studying Jesus in particular, as demonstrated by the ancient heresy of Docetism. When early Greek readers concentrated exclusively on the deity of Jesus, they *de facto* denied Jesus's humanity to be of any real value. But when Docetism reduces the humanity of Christ to an appearance or a metaphor, the meaning of the incarnation is lost.

Equally unhelpful in an opposite direction is an Ebionite reading of Scripture, that is, reading the Bible *only* as a human, historical, and literary object but certainly not the divine word *within* human words.

1. Lewis, *Reflections on the Psalms*, 14.

Lewis counsels an incarnational approach, reading the Old Testament neither as only divine nor as merely human but as irreducibly both. By this approach we read the Bible as a book human as "any other literature" and respect its variety as chronicles, poems, moral/political diatribes, or romances. We also read it as a divine book that God has breathed into and so is "all taken into the service of God's word."[2] That is, the humanity of the text is not passed over nor gilded but "taken up" as a vehicle to bear the word of God in a way corresponding to the Chalcedonian creed. God became human, we are taught, "Not by the conversion of the godhead into flesh, but by taking the manhood into God."[3] Similarly, as various literary forms are "taken up" for God's special purposes, there can be no simple, one-size-fits-all formula for how each in turn is used. Lewis suspects they are "*not all, [used] I suppose, in the same way.*" Upon all forms—poetry, narrative, chronicle—Lewis senses "a Divine pressure." Nevertheless, the human qualities show through, including the less-than-flattering qualities. "Naivety, error, contradiction, even (as in the cursing Psalms) wickedness are not removed."[4]

Naivety? Yes, I suppose this could add a quaint, even innocent charm to ancient narrative. But error and wickedness? What kind of inspired document is this? The kind that embraces the human limitations embedded in the text, limitations that may include simple factual error but that extend to the *inhumanity* of the human authors as well. We are invited to receive the entire package in which the "total result" is "the Word of God," but:

> Not "the Word of God" in the sense that every passage, in itself, gives impeccable science or history. It carries the Word of God; and we (under grace, with attention to tradition and interpreters wiser than ourselves, and with the use of such intelligence and learning as we may have) receive that word from it not by using it as an encyclopedia or an encyclical but by steeping ourselves in its tone or temper and so learning its over-all message.[5]

Something counterintuitive is going on here, as Lewis acknowledges, but he is convinced we mustn't substitute the word preferred for the word

2. Ibid., 94.

3. Ibid., 97.

4. Ibid., 94.

5. Ibid.

that's been given. Indeed, many of us may prefer a different kind of divine disclosure, "an unrefracted light giving us ultimate truth in systematic form"—something we can tabulate, memorize, and rely on like a divine multiplication table. Lewis says he respects, and at moments envies, both the fundamentalist's view of the Bible and the Roman Catholic's view of the Church.[6] Nevertheless, appealing as they may be, Lewis thinks them *insufficiently open* to the word that actually has been given.

Take, for example, Jesus's own teachings. They do not come to us "in that cut and dried, fool-proof, systematic fashion we might have expected or desired. He wrote no book." Christ's own words "cannot be grasped by the intellect alone, cannot be 'got up' as if it were a 'subject.'"[7]

So also with St. Paul. Lewis wonders aloud why did God not grant the church's greatest theologian the gift of clarity. The answer lies in the same direction, so that we learn to respond to the gospel message with the whole person, not the intellect only. Reading Jesus's words embedded in the gospel narratives involves "steeping oneself in a personality, acquiring a new outlook and temper, breathing a new atmosphere, suffering Him, in His own way, to rebuild in us the defaced image of himself."[8] A personal word spoken to us calls for a response in kind. "No net less wide than a man's whole heart, nor less fine of mesh than love, will hold the sacred Fish."[9]

Such a reading of the Psalms refuses to filter out the human error, moral failure, and "wickedness," because when we do, we do not embrace the text so much as dance around it. Let us think of reading as a listening process: when our receptivity trains itself to muffle imperfections, we train ourselves to tune out rather than tune in. When we airbrush away imperfections in the text, the reader actually manufactures a quasi-word of God rather than encounters the flesh and blood text before us. But docetic reading habits have repeatedly interrupted a radical receptivity, not just of the Psalms but of the entire Old Testament. Instead we have used the text to create a domesticated encyclopedia of divine instruction.

But suppose God's revelation includes shadows, including the wickedness of the ancient Hebrew community? Suppose, says Lewis:

6. Ibid.

7. Ibid., 95.

8. Ibid., 96.

9. Ibid., 100.

The value of the OT may be dependent on what seems its imperfection. It may repel one use in order that we may be forced to use it in another way—to find the Word in it, not without repeated and leisurely reading nor without discriminations made by our conscience and our critical faculties, to re-live, while we read, the whole Jewish experience of God's gradual and graded self-revelation, to feel the very contentions between the Word and the human material through which it works. For here again, it is our total response that has to be elicited.[10]

POETRY: THE CURSING PSALMS

All the preceding interpretive guidance is offered in the final chapter of Lewis's book on the Psalms. Chapter by chapter he has wrestled with one challenging text after another. But no Psalms are more awkward to read as God's word than the cursing Psalms. May we dare read them without a docetic filter that strains God's word from amidst the curses? To keep this discussion connected to the actual dilemma, let us survey some of the cursing verses:

May his days be few; May another take his place of leadership. May his children be fatherless. And his wife a widow. May his children be wandering beggars; May they be driven from their ruined homes. May a creditor seize all he has; May strangers plunder the fruits of his labor. May no one extend kindness to him or take pity on his fatherless Children. May his descendants be cut off, their names blotted out from the next generation. May the iniquity of his fathers be remembered before the Lord; May the sin of his mother never be blotted out. May their sins always remain before the Lord, That he may cut off the memory of them from the earth (Ps 109).

Sometimes the curses surprise us, as when they show up in places that are otherwise full of praise. Take Psalm 139:19: "Wilt thou not slay the wicked, O God?"—"as if," says Lewis, "it were surprising that such a simple remedy for human ills had not occurred to the Almighty."[11] But something darker is offered in Psalm 137: "O Daughter of Babylon, doomed to destruction, happy is he who repays you for what you have done to us—he who seizes your infants and dashes them against the rocks"

10. Ibid., 96.
11. Ibid., 24.

(Ps 137:8–9). How does such a poem with sentiment like this "teach, correct, rebuke and train us in righteousness" (2 Tim 3:16)?

Lewis's answer is to "receive" the text, warts and all. First, this means to understand that the Psalmist is almost certainly responding to rather than initiating wickedness. But once Babylon's aggression has planted its poison in the writer, it's no good pretending it isn't there. The Psalmist's appropriate sense of outrage at evil unfortunately has led him directly to thinking "one's own worst passions are holy."[12] The text discloses with painful clarity the natural result of injuring another human being. Moreover, Israel's proximity to God means new possibilities of evil as well as good accompany her. "The higher, the more in danger . . . Of all bad men religious bad men are the worst."[13] When the righteous take it upon themselves to hate God's enemies, they play a fatal game that leads straight to Pharisaism. Hence the cursing in the Psalms exposes a tragedy. As Lewis points out, we know it's profoundly natural to hate those who do us harm. But we know from Scripture itself that it is profoundly wrong, as numerous texts from the OT remind us: "Thou shalt not hate thy brother in thine heart (Lev. 19:17) . . . If thou meet thine enemy's ox or his ass going astray, thou shalt surely bring it back to him (Ex. 23:4,5) . . . Rejoice not when thine enemy falleth, and let not thine heart be glad when he stumbleth (Prov. 24:17) . . . If thine enemy hunger, give him bread (Prov. 25:21)."[14]

If beyond all the brokenness and learned malice, all Scripture is profitable for reproof and correction in righteousness, then it also contains a mercifully severe warning for readers today. To put it bluntly, unless we learn to pray with Christ, "forgive us our debts as we forgive our debtors," every act of injury or cruelty we suffer will infect us with the same passion for revenge and shall inflame the same desires to hallow retaliation as holy. The cursing texts warn me of the trajectory of my own soul toward Pharisaism every time I indulge in hatred or fantasize revenge "if I ever get a chance" because that opportunity may just come. Perhaps due to power differentials at work, I come home and displace my revenge, so to speak, by kicking the dog. But the transplanted annoyance or anger I inflict on those closest to me can deform my domestic world. Reading Psalm 137 reminds and alerts me to the way that cruelty attaches itself to others.

12. Ibid., 31.

13. Ibid., 29, 32.

14. Ibid., 27–8.

Here then is how Lewis reads the cursing Psalms to "edify" today, with all their warts of malice fully on the table. This is, after all, Lewis's agenda—to read the Old Testament Scripture as God's redemptive and renewing word. "To reach the voice of God in the cursing psalms through all the horrible distortions of the human medium, I have gained something . . . the shadows have indicated . . . something more about the light . . ."[15] Given their nature as the speech of the heart, the Psalms express before God our human emotional polarities, both heights and shadows. Lewis invites us to listen to the entirety as revelatory.

Now let us ask: what can we take from this exercise in listening to Scripture as God's voice through the "horrible distortions" of the human medium in *poetry* that helps us listen to God's voice through *historical narrative*? As with the Psalms, what happens when we set aside the filters that omit "naivety, error, and downright wickedness"? First, let us consider a text regularly whitewashed of its shadows.

NARRATIVE: ON PUTTING DOWN THE KNIFE

> After these things God tested Abraham. He said to him, "Abraham!" And he said, "Here I am." He said, "Take your son, your only son Isaac, whom you love, and go to the land of Moriah, and offer him there as a burnt offering on one of the mountains that I shall show you . . . When they came to the place that God had shown him, Abraham built an altar there and laid the wood in order. He bound his son Isaac, and laid him on the altar, on top of the wood. Then Abraham reached out his hand and took the knife to kill his son. But the angel of the LORD called to him from heaven, and said, "Abraham, Abraham!" And he said, "Here I am." He said, "Do not lay your hand on the boy or do anything to him; for now I know that you fear God, since you have not withheld your son, your only son, from me." And Abraham looked up and saw a ram, caught in a thicket by its horns. Abraham went and took the ram and offered it up as a burnt offering instead of his son (Gen 22:1–2, 9–14).

It is unlikely that this is simply a glib morality tale encapsulated by the wooden formula, "Abraham hears God. Abraham obeys God. *Ergo* God rewards Abraham." At some elementary level, there may be something quite simple going on, but there are other levels and dark questions nearby

---

15. Ibid., 96. Cf. also 113 where Lewis discusses further positive uses of the Psalm as an allegory of discipline against our tendencies toward self-indulgence.

that mustn't be avoided. Suppose, as do many commentators, that child sacrifice was a well-known feature of Israel's neighbors. What if, by God's interruption of this ritual, the story exposes all child sacrifice as evil, even when cloaked in divine authority? The text thus narrates how Abraham, and through him all of Israel for all time, has been granted a deep insight into God's character. Unlike the close-by gods of Moloch, there are sacrifices Israel's God will never require and which are never holy. We are glad to learn this, of course, but we are bound to ask why God would suggest such cruelty in the first place. Or to put the question the other way round, does the text provide any clues as to how Abraham discovered that Israel's God would never demand such vicious piety?

The rabbi and psychologist Michael Lerner has called attention to a probing insight from ancient Hebrew Midrash. The Midrash notices that when God tells Abraham to sacrifice his son Isaac, the Hebrew denotes *Elohim* (the generic term for God) as the speaker. But when the story reaches its climax, the text explicitly tells us it is *Yahweh's angel—not Elohim*—who tells Abraham not to harm the child. The rabbi asks, "Has Abraham perhaps some difficulty distinguishing the voice of the cultural expectations from the true voice of God?"[16] Once Abraham puts down the knife, he sees a ram caught in a thicket nearby and so inaugurates the ritual substitution of animals for humans. A redemptive substitute has been provided. It shall remain for the New Testament to disclose in the fullness of time how, once and for all, a redemptive substitution shall be made on behalf of all Abraham's children.

For the reader seeking to hear God's voice, the point is this: if Abraham struggled to distinguish the voice of the true God from the internalized voice of cultural expectations (the unconscious, as Lerner puts it), how much harder is this task today? The text suggests this discernment may not be as simple as we might wish. Were it not for the downright intervention of Yahweh's angel, Abraham's piety could easily have been indistinguishable from the disciples of Moloch.

That is the tragedy pondered by the young British war poet, Wilfred Owen, as he meditated upon this ancient text in the trenches of World War I.

> So Abram rose, and clave the wood, and went,
> And took the fire with him, and a knife.

16. Lerner, *Jewish Renewal*, 45.

> And as they sojourned both of them together,
> Isaac the first-born spake and said, My Father,
> Behold the preparations, fire and iron,
> But where the lamb for this burnt-offering?
> Then Abram bound the youth with belts and straps,
> And builded parapets and trenches there,
> And stretched forth the knife to slay his son.
> When lo! An angel called him out of heaven,
> Saying, Lay not thy hand upon the lad,
> Neither do anything to him. Behold,
> A ram, caught in a thicket by its horns;
> Offer the Ram of Pride instead of him.
> But the old man would not so, but slew his son,
> And half the seed of Europe, one by one.[17]

Behold, says Wilfred Owen, the willingness of Europe's old men to sacrifice their children in battle—with the Christian churches as eager handmaids, chaplains as guarantors of God's blessing on the troops. Nearly a century later we still shake our heads at the blood-drenched numbers: ten million soldiers killed on the battlefield; a further twenty million dead from war-related injuries, illnesses, and diseases. Even the United States, having waited three years to enter the killing fields, lost more than one hundred thousand soldiers. Despite these horrific numbers and the passing of a century to reflect, how many nations have really grown weary of sending off their youth to the immolations of war? There remains no lack of religious assurance that "God" is with us, that "our" sacrifice is noble. The lethal consequences of patriotism married to piety were the shadows Wilfred Owen grappled in his day as he meditated on the sources of his faith tradition, searching for wisdom. One can read his poem as evidence that he also was seeking a way to distinguish between the voice of Abraham's God and that of the nations' gods who were piously offering up their children.

Similar shadows and wickedness hover over our world today. While recent decades offer increasing hope that Europe (after two world wars in twenty years) has begun to turn its swords into ploughshares, vast regions of the world remain enamored by the sword. Meanwhile, the quality of each nation's future hinges on whether it begins to heed Yahweh's angel and lays down its knives.

17. Owen, cf. www.poemtree.com/poems/ParableOfTheOldMan.htm. Cf. Williams, *On Christian Theology*, 30.

READING OLD AND NEW TESTAMENT SIDE BY SIDE:
DEUTERONOMY 7:1–2; MATTHEW 15:21–28

When the LORD your God brings you into the land that you are entering to take possession of it, and clears away many nations before you, the Hittites, the Girgashites, the Amorites, the Canaanites, the Perizzites, the Hivites and the Jebushites, seven nations more numerous and mightier than yourselves, and when the LORD your God gives them over to you, and you defeat them, then you must devote them to complete destruction. You shall make no covenant with them and show no mercy to them (Deut 7:1–2).

And Jesus went away from there and withdrew to the district of Tyre and Sidon. And behold, a Canaanite woman from that region came out and was crying, "Have mercy on me, O Lord, Son of David; my daughter is severely oppressed by a demon." But he did not answer her a word. And his disciples came and begged him, saying, "Send her away, for she is crying out after us." He answered, "I was sent to the lost sheep of the house of Israel." But she came and knelt before him, saying, "Lord, help me." And he answered, "It is not right to take the children's bread and throw it to the dogs." She said, "Yes, Lord, yet even the dogs eat the crumbs that fall from their masters' table." Then Jesus answered her, "O woman, great is your faith! Be it done for you as you desire." And her daughter was healed instantly (Matt 15:21–28).

Let us apply a warts-and-all receptivity by laying an Old Testament and New Testament narrative alongside one another and consider how *together*, not apart, they offer fresh meaning. I know conservative Christians who cite Deuteronomy as the reason why the modern state of Israel must not compromise in any land for peace negotiations with Palestinians. Moreover, the "rules of engagement" can rightfully include pre-emptive strikes into Gaza, massive retaliation, and even the Deuteronomy solution itself, though this is more diplomatically spoken of as "transfer" of the local population. All this is justified under the authoritative word of Deuteronomy: "Show no mercy." Scripture tells how Israel (with one or two exceptions) did precisely that. "As soon as the people heard the sound of the trumpets, they raised a great shout, and the wall fell down flat; so the people of God charged straight ahead into the city and captured it. Then they devoted to destruction by the edge of the sword all in the city, both men and women, young and old, oxen, sheep, and donkeys"

(Josh 6:20–22). Though many (by no means all) within the evangelical and fundamentalist schools do not hesitate to make this text a pretext for contemporary Middle Eastern strategy, I suggest we follow a twofold approach, which echoes Lewis: acknowledge the wickedness and look to the New Testament for evidence of a *transposition* of both the promise of land and the method of acquisition.

Matthew's text suggests such a transformative moment. Here is a Messiah who untwists Israel's attitude toward her despised neighbors from merciless to merciful. Grant LeMarquand has thoughtfully explored the symbolic implications of this encounter alongside the conquest narrative, so I will draw on his research at several points in what follows.[18] This text contains the sole reference to a Canaanite in the New Testament. (Perhaps this is evidence for the extreme Jewish distaste for a people deemed more odious even than Samaritans.) The context itself suggests it as a defining moment; it comes in the middle of the two wilderness feedings that occur in Galilee, a place Matthew describes as "Galilee of the Gentiles" (4:15). Jesus's ministry here pushes the boundaries toward a very non-Jewish atmosphere, as well as a transformed approach to these long-despised neighbors. In the feeding that follows, the seven baskets left over may suggest the perfection of fulfillment, a fulfillment that includes Gentiles. What a shock for the "set apart" to witness how Jesus's ministry brings near to the covenant these unclean Gentile dogs! In book after book of the New Testament, each in its own way, this is the inevitable trajectory of Jesus's ministry. Yes, he ministers first to the house of Israel. But he will relentlessly pursue Israel's intended vocation to be light to Gentiles.

The moment of alteration starts as the woman directly pleads, "Have mercy on me, O Lord, Son of David; my daughter is severely oppressed by a demon" (v. 22). If we juxtapose her words with Deuteronomy's clear command to the Israelites regarding the Canaanites: "Show no mercy to them," the time is at hand to revisit the ancient curse. How shall Jesus respond? When we read words of extermination in Deuteronomy 7, do they sound any less cruel in narrative than the poetic cry for violent revenge in the Psalms? Spoken in prose, the cruelty seems only heightened. Jesus's opponents regularly accuse him of destroying Israel's heritage: setting aside the temple, the law, and the external features of covenant practice. What about the promise of land to Abraham? Will Jesus also transpose

---

18. LeMarquand, "The Canaanite Conquest of Jesus (Mt 15:21–28)," 237–47.

this ingredient of Israel's hope? "You have heard it said of old . . . but I say unto you . . ."

CRUMBS FOR A CANAANITE

Now comes a despised descendant of the despised Canaanites humbly requesting help from David's Son. The strangest of conversations follows, not something a gospel writer could have made up were they not eye-witnesses.[19] While it would be useful to have a sermon or an essay from Lewis on this eccentric conversation between Jesus and the Canaanite, we are fortunate enough to have a sermon of George Macdonald's, the nineteenth-century Scottish preacher and novelist to whom Lewis frequently acknowledged his spiritual debt.[20]

Let us suppose the Deuteronomy text and its legacy presses on Jesus's mind and heart, its shadows reinforcing this ancient resistance to offer mercy. Indeed, here Jesus recapitulates the historical denigration of Canaanites, first by avoiding her, then by virtually insulting her. What is going on? MacDonald insists that Jesus uses her presence as the needle point in time to lance the boil of his disciples' pride in their racial/cultural superiority. "For their sakes this chosen Gentile must be pained a little further, must bear with her Saviour her part of suffering for the redemption even of his chosen apostles."[21] In other words, Jesus's initial coldness toward the woman's earnest request models temporarily the disciples' own sense of racial/religious superiority, in order that he might "arouse in them the disapproval of their own exclusiveness by putting it on for a moment that they might see it apart from themselves."[22]

When the disciples ask Jesus to send her away, it is a "request for Jesus to give her some sort of uncovenanted mercy" so they don't have to watch her grieve her daughter any longer. In this embarrassingly minimalist way, they advocate for her before Israel's Messiah. But Jesus will not let them off with their pride intact. He wants them to bear a little longer with what it must feel like to be an object of their miserly compassion.

---

19. Wright, *Matthew for Everyone, Part 1*, 201.

20. Cf. MacDonald, *George MacDonald, An Anthology*, 18. "I know hardly any other writer who seems to be closer, or more continually close, to the Spirit of Christ Himself."

21. MacDonald, *The Miracles of Our Lord*, 131.

22. Ibid., 132.

"It is not right to take the children's bread and to throw it to the dogs."
Jesus gives voice to the feelings that Jews felt "that the elect Jews about
him might begin to understand that in him is neither Jew nor Gentile, but
all are brethren."[23] The woman's humble reply, "Yet even the dogs eat the
crumbs that fall from the master's table," ends the dialogue and provokes
Jesus's full and unconditional healing of her beloved daughter. Only in
Jesus's words to the woman can the healing desperately required by his
own followers finally emerge.

> Where, O disciples, are your children and your dogs now? Is not
> the wall of partition henceforth destroyed? No; you too have to be
> made whole of a worse devil, that of personal and national pride,
> before you understand.[24]

The text is revealing something mysterious; a glimpse of Jesus internally untwisting from within his own little flock the natural ethnic Jewish
antipathy toward the Canaanite people. MacDonald supposes he dons
temporarily the Jewish mantle of superiority and disapproval so that the
disciples can see just how it looks and feels to the suffering Canaanite,
grieving for her child. Small wonder they could not forget his awkward
words and recorded them faithfully.

It is possible that Jesus's threefold refusal echoes the ancient test
of Ruth, the Moabite, who showed her serious intentions of joining her
mother-in-law by refusing to be refused.[25] Be that as it may, the result is
clear: the Canaanite woman had been shown mercy, a mercy not strained
by any racial or cultural privilege. This lone woman anticipated the coming of many from the east and the west to eat with Abraham, Isaac, and
Jacob in heaven's kingdom (Matt 8:11). If we couple this with the feeding
of Gentiles in the wilderness (in contrast to the Hebrews being singu-
larly attended to in the wilderness by Moses), then Matthew is describing
the coming of a radical new Exodus. Hence here is a new entry into the
promised land that doesn't subjugate or exterminate Canaanites but receives them as co-recipients of mercy, for in Christ's advancing kingdom
those who extend mercy do so as a free response, mirroring the manner
in which they have been received.

23. Ibid., 135.

24. Ibid., 137.

25. Ruth 1:16, cf. LeMarquand, *The Canaanite Conquest of Jesus*, 2.

Please note what has happened to the conquest of Canaan in which no mercy is shown and extermination is the prescribed method of cleansing; it has gone the way of the Messiah who redeems Israel *sans* military victory over her enemies. Messiah Jesus offers himself as the sacrifice, the suffering servant of Isaiah 53 who dies in a shameful way, for *both Jews and Gentiles*, extending the holiest cup of mercy even to Canaanites. Behold the strange Joshua who leads his disciples into a promised land turned upside down.

When we acknowledge the shadows, the coming light shines more boldly. We should not airbrush Joshua's order that every non-Hebrew man, woman, child, and animal be slaughtered and burned, all in the name of Israel's God. Paul has already told us that God gave the good law as gift to Israel but that she misused the law for self-privilege instead of service to her neighbors and Creator (Rom 2). Thus, says Paul, his own people will be judged by their deeds, as will the Gentiles. So in this light we must ask: did Israel, in the very act of taking the land, mis-take it? The prophetic witness is not shy in declaring that eventually Israel's deeds led to her removal from the land. Where is the evidence that Israel started out superbly? Israel's story suggests instead a complicated but consistent portrait of worshipping false and distorted images (idols) of God. Jesus, the one true high priest, King David's greater son, the greatest prophet, climactically discloses both the extent of Israel's idolatry as well as God's covenantal mercies by offering himself on her behalf, both priest and victim, who offers true and acceptable worship once and for all.

A CONTEMPORARY RESPONSE: PALESTINE AND ISRAEL

Oskar Pfister, the Swiss pastor and friend of Freud, once remarked that you can tell a lot about someone by how they read the Bible. Today in the Middle East or in circles of Washington DC, there are readers for whom Deuteronomy 7 is sufficient reason to conquer the enemy or "liberate" the people, according to our blueprint for freedom. "Show no mercy," says the text. "Go and do thou likewise," hears the avenger. But readers who listen to Matthew's story *alongside* Deuteronomy sense that when Jesus hears and grants the Canaanite woman's plea, he has altered Israel's true path forever.

What is the unfinished response for Christ's disciples who read this text today? For a start, let us begin to *wonder* what it means to bear witness to Jesus's transformation of the ancient Jewish/Canaanite rivalry. At the level of personal and private analogy, there are implications aplenty for our domestic worlds. Is there a Canaanite neighbor I have contemptuously avoided or dehumanized? Can God be asking me to express mercy in their hour of need?

We began this study by learning how Mary's Magnificat teaches us to reconnect the personal world of families and the public life of nations. This text offers us a continuing summons to apply crumbs-for-Gentile-dog lenses to where the ancestral fires of ethnic and religious hatred are still bursting in flames. Writing as a citizen of the United States, I am compelled to ask: how can I bear witness to Christ's vision to embrace Canaanites as well as Jews, excluding neither Israel nor her Palestinian neighbors, from the covenant blessings of mercy in today's Middle East? Unfortunately since 1948, Western politicians seem to have never imagined that a Middle East policy could be based on the notions of inclusion or reconciliation. Instead, *Realpolitik* seems only to envision separatist "two-state" solutions that easily morph into separate and unequal "Bantustan/Canton" solutions imposed by whoever owns the largest armory. The strategies of separate development are now more than half a century old and show no sign of resolving either the hatred on display in Psalm 137 or the lingering prejudice of Matthew 15.

But suppose the mercy shown to the Canaanite woman subverts the conquest narrative's privileged priority once and for all? Suppose a *Magnificat* lens invites us to imagine how this text might reconstruct international relations grounded in reconciliation rather than conquest and division?[26] A gospel that has implications for public life and history, not just a private individual redemption, has yet to write its chapter on history's pages, but when it does, it will declare good news for *both* Canaanites *and* Jews in the Middle East. Christ's strategy here is the key for which public history waits in travail.

We began this chapter with a quotation by which Lewis launched *Reflections on the Psalms* with the hope of avoiding controversial questions as much as possible. Now we end this chapter and this book with a controversy. I have led us along this path not because I wish to depart from Lewis's strategy (though some controversies are unavoidable), nor because I am in less need of my opponents' prayers and goodwill than

26. A good place to begin further study of this question is Bailey's seminal essay, "St. Paul's Understanding of the Territorial Promise of God to Abraham." For further study see also Chapman, *Whose Land of Promise?* and Burge, *Whose Land? Whose Promise?*

Lewis, but because the vision of these two women and their witness to the gospel seem the fitting bookends for this study: Mary's vision of public life is not divorced from personal salvation, and the Canaanite woman's plea for inclusion in God's covenant mercies is no longer delayed.

Given Jesus's unusual negotiation with her, we are no doubt left a fair bit of latitude to ask: how might the healing of ethnic warfare and superiority/inferiority identity take place in our world today? For believers, this brings to mind the vision of peace described by St. Paul:

> For Christ himself has brought us peace by making Jews and Gentiles one people. With his own body he broke down the wall that separated them and kept them enemies . . . By his death on the cross Christ destroyed their enmity; by means of the cross he united both races into one body and brought them back to God (Eph 2:14, 16).

Lewis would remind us that simply longing for peace on earth (for God's will to be done on earth as it is in heaven) is no guarantee that you and I will live to see communities of Israeli settlers sitting down at table with Hamas politicians. But let us recall the German youth walking home that morning dazed from a tragic watch and the "what if" connection of his identity with the English family returning home during the London Blitz. These connections exist only in our imaginations when today's rivals are busy reloading for business as usual. But we wait, in prayer and action, for the day the entire world will see and feel the connection and be moved to reshape the boundaries of their hearts and their lands. This moment may not come until our children or grandchildren or great-grandchildren's time. Until then, creation and too many wounded children and grandchildren will continue their groaning and longing for that day. But that day will come. For to paraphrase Lewis, it would be a peculiar world where the yearning for reconciliation is no clue to the world's true future.[27]

CONCLUSION

One of the best gifts in reading the Bible with C. S. Lewis is tasting his enthusiasm for how Christ's words and deeds were never meant simply to be preserved in a spiritual museum called the Bible or the church, but have always been intended for implementation. Whether we dwell

27. Lewis, "The Weight of Glory," 99.

in "Greenland's icy mountains" threatened with global warming or "England's green and pleasant land," bedeviled by dark, satanic mills, we cannot rest, as Blake foresaw, "Till we have built Jerusalem."[28] If we read with no intention of being caught up ourselves along with our world into a lived narrative of transformation, we empty Scripture of its meaning, cutting ourselves off from our true humanity and deforming ourselves into something never intended. We mirror the verdict Lewis pronounces in calling us back from the abyss:

> We are half hearted creatures, fooling about with drink and sex and ambition when infinite joy is offered us, like an ignorant child who wants to go on making mud pies in a slum because he cannot imagine what is meant by the offer of a holiday at the sea. We are far too easily pleased.[29]

Perhaps this is why it is so important that sinners-in-training-to-be-saints do not read the Bible in isolation but are gladly accompanied by the church, whose prophets, scholars, witnesses, and martyrs, through time and eternity, join us as we seek wisdom in learning how to read and respond to the text. This is why we join with Lewis and a cloud of other saints, connected by the feeling intellect to indwell the text, and its cultural/historical background. We do this not to agree with everything Lewis and the saints have written, nor to vainly repeat their ideas word for word. But surrounded by their witness, we dare to read the text, trusting their anticipation of true beauty restored, hoping that if their soiled hearts can be cleansed, so can ours. With hands, heads, and hearts outstretched, we join them in Jesus's project to love the world until his Father's will is done on earth as in heaven.

Tolle, lege; tolle, lege.

28. Blake, "And Did Those Feet" 83.
29. Lewis, "The Weight of Glory," 94–5.

Bibliography

Augustine, *The City of God*. New York: Image Books, 1958.

Baker, Leo. "Near the Beginning" in *C. S. Lewis at the Breakfast Table*, edited by James T. Como, 3–10. London: Collins, 1980.

Bailey, Kenneth E. *Jesus Through Middle Eastern Eyes, Cultural Studies in the Gospels*. Downer's Grove, IL: IVP, 2008.

———. "St. Paul's Understanding of the Territorial Promise of God to Abraham (Romans 4:13 in its Historical/Theological Context)," *The Near East School of Theology, Theological Review*. Volume 15, No. 1 (1994), 59–69.

———. *The Cross and the Prodigal*. St. Louis, MO: Concordia Press, 1973.

Barth, Karl. *Church Dogmatics*. Volume IV/3, part one. Edinburgh, Scotland: T & T Clark, 1976.

———. "Schleiermacher's Celebration of Christmas." In *Theology and Church, Shorter Writings 1920–1928*, translated by Louise Pettibone Smith, 136–58. New York: Harper and Row: 1962.

———. *The Epistle to the Romans*. New York: Oxford University Press, 1972.

Bediako, Kwame. *Jesus and the Gospel in Africa*. Maryknoll, NY: Orbis, 2004.

Begbie, Jeremy. *Resounding Truth*. Grand Rapids, MI: Baker, 2007.

Blake, William. "And Did Those Feet" in *The Norton Anthology of English Literature*. Volume 1, edited by M. H. Abrams, et al., 183. New York: W. & W. Norton and Company, 1968.

Brown, Dan. *The Da Vinci Code*. New York: Doubleday, 2003.

Burge, Gary. *Whose Land? Whose Promise?*. Cleveland, OH: The Pilgrim Press, 2003.

Campbell, John McLeod. *The Nature of the Atonement*. London: Macmillan and Co., 1895.

Casey, Michael. *Sacred Reading, the Ancient Art of Lectio Divina*. Ligouri, MO: Liguori Publications, 1995.

Chacour, Fr. Elias. Online http://www.pilgrimsofibillin.org, Summer 2006.

Chapman, Colin. *Whose Land of Promise?* Grand Rapids, MI: Baker, 2002.

Christensen, Michael J. *C. S. Lewis on Scripture*. Waco, TX: Word Books, 1979.

Coleridge, Samuel Taylor. *Biographia Literaria*. Chapter XIV, *The Norton Anthology of English Literature*. Volume 2, edited by M. H. Abrams, et al., 273–9. New York: W. W. Norton and Company, 1968.

Chesterton, G. K. *What's Wrong with the World*. New York: Dodd, Mead, and Company, 1910.

Donne, John. "Death Be Not Proud." In *Holy Sonnets. The Norton Anthology of English Literature*. Volume 1, edited by M. H. Abrams, et al., 909. New York: W.W. Norton and Company, 1968.

Freston, Paul. "Contours of Latin American Pentecostalism." In *Christianity Reborn*, edited by Donald M. Lewis, 224. Grand Rapids, MI: Eerdmans, 2004.

Gandhi, Mohandas K. *Autobiography: The Story of My Experiments with Truth*. New York: Dover, 1983.

Gettman, Tom. John Woolman Peacemaking Lecture. November 7, 2005. George Fox University. Newberg, OR.

Green, Roger Lancelyn and Walter Hooper. *C.S. Lewis, A Biography*. New York: Harcourt Brace Jovanovich, 1974.

Gunton, Colin. *The Actuality of the Atonement*. London: T & T Clark, 1998.

Hoover, A. J. *God, Germany and Britain in the Great War, a Study in Clerical Nationalism*. Westport, CT: Praeger, 1989.

Hooper, Walter, editor. *They Stand Together. The Letters of C. S. Lewis to Arthur Greeves* (1914–1963). London: Collins, 1979.

Irenaeus. *Against Heresies*. 446, 448. *Ante-Nicene Fathers 1*. Peabody, MA: Hendrickson Publishers, 1994.

Kalu, Ogbu. Review of "Pentecostalism in a Globalising, African Economy," 160. In *International Bulletin Missionary Research*, Volume 29, no. 3.

Keillor, Garrison. *Lake Wobegon Days*. New York: Penguin, 1986.

LaHaye, Tim and Jerry B. Jenkins. *Left Behind*. Carol Stream, IL: Tyndale House, 1998.

Lasch, Christopher. *Culture of Narcissism*. New York: W. W. Norton Company and Ltd., 1979.

LeMarquand, Grant. "The Canaanite Conquest of Jesus (Mt 15:21–28)." In *Essays in Honour of Frederik Wisse: Scholar, Churchman, Mentor*, edited by Warren Kappeler, 237–47. *ARC: The Journal of the Faculty of Religious Studies*, McGill University 33 (2005).

Lerner, Michael. *Jewish Renewal*. New York: G. P. Putnam's Sons, 1994.

Lewis, C. S. *The Abolition of Man*, New York: Macmillan, 1962.

——. "Bluspels and Flalansferes, a Semantic Nightmare." In *Rehabilitations and Other Essays*, 133–58. London: Oxford University Press, 1939.

——. "The Case for Christianity." In *Mere Christianity*, 7–62 New York: MacMillan, 1969.

——. *English Literature in the Sixteenth Century*. Oxford: Oxford University Press, 1973.

——. "Equality," in *Present Concerns*, edited by Walter Hooper, 18, 20. New York: Harcourt, Brace, and Jovanovitch, 1986.

——. *An Experiment in Criticism*, Cambridge: Cambridge University Press, 1961.

——. *The Four Loves*. New York: Harcourt, Brace, and Jovanovitch, 1960.

——. *The Great Divorce*. London: Geoffrey Bles, 1946.

——. "The Great Sin." In *Mere Christianity*, 108–14. New York: MacMillan. 1969.

——. *The Horse and His Boy*. London: Puffin Books, 1978.

——. "The Humanitarian Theory of Punishment." *God in the Dock*, edited by Walter Hooper, 294. Grand Rapids, MI: Eerdmans, 1970.

——. "The Inner Ring." In *Screwtape Proposes a Toast and Other Pieces*, 28–40. London: Fontana, 1969.

——. *Letters of C. S. Lewis*, edited by W. H. Lewis, New York: Harcourt, Brace, and World, 1966.

——. *Letters to Malcolm, Chiefly on Prayer*. New York: Harcourt, Brace and World, 1964.

——. *The Lion, the Witch, and the Wardrobe*. London: Puffin, 1978.

———. "Love's as Warm as Tears." In *Poems by C. S. Lewis,* edited by Walter Hooper, 123. New York: Harcourt, Brace, and World, Inc. 1964.

———. "On Living in An Atomic Age." In *Present Concerns,* edited by Walter Hooper, 79. New York: Harcourt, Brace, and Jovanovitch, 1986.

———. *The Magician's Nephew.* London: Puffin Books, 1978.

———. *Miracles, A Preliminary Study.* London: Collins, 1966.

———. "Myth Became Fact." In *God in the Dock,* edited by Walter Hooper, 67. Grand Rapids: Eerdmans, 1970.

———. *Out of the Silent Planet.* New York: Collier Books, 1962.

———. *Perelandra.* New York: Collier Books, 1962.

———. "The Perfect Penitent." In *Mere Christianity,* 59–61. New York: MacMillan, 1969.

———. *A Preface to Paradise Lost.* New York: Oxford University Press, 1969.

———. *Prince Caspian.* London: Puffin, 1977.

———. *The Problem of Pain.* New York: MacMillan, 1972.

———. *Reflections on the Psalms.* London: Fontana, 1969

———. *The Screwtape Letters.* London: Collins Fontana, 1971.

———. *Selected Literary Essays.* Cambridge: Cambridge University Press, 1969.

———. "Social Morality." In *Mere Christianity,* 78–83. New York: MacMillan, 1969.

———. "Sometimes Fairy Stories May Say Best What's To Be Said." In *Of Other Worlds, Essays and Stories,* edited by Walter Hooper, 37. New York: Harcourt, Brace, and World, 1966.

———. *Studies in Medieval and Renaissance Literature.* Cambridge: Cambridge University Press, 1966.

———. *Studies in Words.* Cambridge: Cambridge University Press, 1975.

———. *Surprised by Joy.* London: Geoffrey Bles Ltd, 1955.

———. *Till We Have Faces: A Myth Retold.* Grand Rapids, MI: William B. Eerdmans, 1970.

———. "Transposition." In *Screwtape Proposes a Toast,* 77. London: Collins Fontana, 1969.

———. *The Voyage of the Dawn Treader.* London: Puffin, 1978.

———. "We Have Cause to Be Uneasy." In *Mere Christianity,* 36–9. New York: MacMillan, 1969.

———. "We Have No Right to Happiness." In *God in the Dock.* Edited by Walter Hooper, 322. Grand Rapids, MI: Eerdmans, 1970.

———. "The Weight of Glory." In *Screwtape Proposes a Toast and Other Pieces,* 94–111. London: 1969.

McGann, Jerome J. Editor. *The Complete Writings and Pictures of Dante Gabriel Rossetti.* Online http://www.rossettiarchive.org/zoom/s44.img.html

MacDonald, George. *George MacDonald, An Anthology,* edited by C. S. Lewis. London: Geoffrey Bles, 1946.

———. *The Miracles of Our Lord.* London: Strahan and Co. (Facsimile by J.J. Flynn), 1987.

———. *Unspoken Sermons.* Series 3. London: Longmans, Green, and Co. (Facsimile by J. J. Flynn), 1987.

Mandela, Nelson, *Long Walk to Freedom.* Boston, MA: Little, Brown, and Company, 1995.

Miller, Donald. "Confession: Coming Out of the Closet." In *Blue Like Jazz,* 113–28. New York: Nelson, 2003.

Newbigin, Lesslie. *A Word in Season*. Grand Rapids, MI: Eerdmans, 1994.

Owen, Wilfred. "Parable of the Old Man and the Young." Online: http://www.poemtree. com/poems/ParableOfTheOldMan.htm.

Ringer, Robert J. *Looking Out for Number 1*. New York: Ballantine Books, 1977.

Robinson, Barbara. *The Best Christmas Pageant Ever*. New York: Harper Collins, 1972.

Ruskin, John. *The Works of John Ruskin*. Volume 33, edited by E. T. Cook and Alexander Wedderburn. London: George Allen. 1908.

Saver, George. *Jack: C. S. Lewis and His Times*. San Francisco, CA: Harper & Row, 1988.

Sayers, Dorothy L. "The Dogma Is the Drama." In *Creed or Chaos?*, 20–4. London: Methuen, 1947.

Smail, Thomas. *The Forgotten Father*. London: Hodder and Stoughton, 1980.

Thielicke, Helmut. *How the World Began*. Philadelphia, PA: Muhlenberg, 1961.

Thiselton, Anthony C. *New Horizons in Hermeneutics*. Grand Rapids, MI: Zondervan, 1992.

Tolkien, J. R. R. *The Lord of the Rings*. London: Unwin, 1978.

———. "On Fairy Stories." In *The Tolkien Reader*, 71–3. New York: Ballantine Books, 1966.

———. *The Letters of J. R. R. Tolkien*, edited by Humphrey Carpenter. London: Allen and Unwin. 1981.

Vaus, Will. *Mere Theology. A Guide to the Thought of C. S. Lewis*. Downers Grove, IL: InterVarsity Press, 2004.

Williams, Charles and Lewis, C. S., "Williams and the Arthuriad." In *Taliessin Through Logres*. Grans Rapids, MI: Eerdmans, 1974.

Wright, N. T. (Tom). *Acts for Everyone, Part 1*. London: SPCK, 2008.

———. *Jesus and the Victory of God*. Minneapolis, MN: Fortress Press, 1996.

———. *Judas and the Gospel of Jesus*. Grand Rapids, MI: Baker Books, 2006.

———. *Matthew for Everyone, Part 1*. London: SPCK, 2002.

———. *Paul for Everyone, Galatians and Thessalonians*. London: SPCK, 2002.

———. *The Millennium Myth*. Louisville, KY: John Knox Press, 1999.

Williams, Rowan. Archbishop of Canterbury New Year's Message, 2006. Holy Trinity Church, Clapham. Online: http://www.archbishopofcanterbury.org/605

———. *On Christian Theology*. Malden, MA: Blackwell, 2001.

The Compact Edition of the Oxford English Dictionary, New York: Oxford University Press, 1971.

Scripture Index

Genesis

Genesis 22:1-2, 9-14   96
Genesis 27:30-35   74

Exodus

Exodus 23:4, 5   95

Leviticus

Leviticus 19:17   95

Deuteronomy

Deuteronomy 7:1-2   99, 100
Deuteronomy 15:4   83

Joshua

Joshua 6:20-22   100

Ruth

Ruth 1:16   102

Psalm

Psalm 19   63, 66, 71, 72
Psalm 109   94
Psalm 137   94
Psalm 139   94

Proverbs

Proverbs 1:7   83
Proverbs 24:17   95
Proverbs 25:21   95

Matthew

Matthew 4:15   100
Matthew 8:11   102
Matthew 10:8   84
Matthew 11:29   81
Matthew 15:21-28   99
Matthew 20:20-28

Luke

Luke 1:26-38   9, 20
Luke 1:51-55   23
Luke 2:34-35   21
Luke 5:8   x

John

John 3:16   60
John 8:31-32   39, 48

Acts

Acts 4:32-5:5   83

Romans

Romans 1:20-23   64, 67, 72
Romans 2:1   69, 103

Romans–continued

Romans 2:17–24	64
Romans 3–5	25
Romans 3:10	27, 30
Romans 3:23	27
Romans 8:15–16	89
Romans 8:17	90
Romans 8:18	105
Romans 8:23–25	
Romans 9–11	74–82

I Corinthians

I Cor. 15:32	34

II Corinthians

II Cor. 12:9–10	57

Galatians

Galatians 4:4–7	39, 48

Ephesians

Ephesians 2:13	81
Ephesians 2:14, 16	105
Ephesians 3:1	42
Ephesians 3:9	42
Ephesians. 3:15	41

II Timothy

II Timothy 3:16	95

I John

I John 1:5	60

Subject/Name Index

A

Ananias and Sapphira 84–90
Anselm 29, 30
Apologetics 54, 57–58,
  as hospitality 56,
  as apology 57,
  as inversion of economic power 58,
  natural theology 65
Aristotle 42, 43
Atonement theory 24–38
  penal substitution 29, 34, 35, 36, 37
  recapitulation 32, 33
Augustine 71
Austin, Jane 15

B

Bacchus 56, 57
Bailey, Kenneth 21, 32, 104
Barfield, Owen 15
Barth, Karl 12, 59
Bediako, Kwame 53, 54, 56
Beowulf 3, 5, 20
Brown, Dan 18
Buddhism 12
Burge, Gary 104
Bultmann, Rudolf 55
C
Calvin 6–7, 29, 30
Calvinism 29, 74
Campbell, J. Macleod 29, 30
Carter, Jimmy 79
Chacour, Elias 72
Chapman, Colin 104
Chesterton, G. K. 59
Christmas 10
Christendom 50–59

Church, *as a school for holiness* 89–90,
  106
Clement of Alexandria 81
Coleridge, S. T. 11
Cursing Psalms 94

D

Docetism 91
Donne, John 34

E

Ebionism 91
Economics, *and Christian mission* 43,
  58, 70
  consumerism 41, 42
  debt relief 45
Election, *doctrine of* 74–82
Enlightenment 10, 21, 57
Edwards, Jonathan 29

F

Fear, *its use in preaching* 88
Feeling intellect x, 3, 19, 29, 45, 48, 106
Freedom 39–48, 59
Freston, Paul 53
Fukuyama, Francis 7

G

Gandhi, Mohandas 26
Gettman, Tom 58
Gifford, Paul 53
Globalization 41, 59
Gnosticism 18–19

Greenspan, Alan 43
Great Britain 51, 67
the Great Dance 50
Greeves, Arthur 25–26
Griffiths, Bede 65
Gunton, Colin 29

H

Harrison, George 12
Hatred, *relative and absolute* 75–77
Hermeneutics ix, 3–6
    contribution of Reformation 6, 16
    devotional reading 13, 17
    dispensationalism 18
    felt attunement 3, 7
    Ignatian method 6
    Indwelling 3–4, 13, 19, 23, 93–96
    Lectio Divina 6
    reading for discipleship 5, 105–6
    reading Old and New Testaments
        together 91, 99–103,
    reading the cursing Psalms 95
    reading narrative 97–98
Hoover, A. J. 60
Human response 8, 15,
Hunt, Holman 22

I

Imagination 18, 65
    baptized imagination 4, 55
Inner Ring 55
Inspiration of Scripture 92
Irenaeus 32, 33, 34
Inversion of hierarchy 51
Islam 54

J

Jacob and Esau 78–81
Justice 27, 31, 54
    restorative justice 31, 32, 37

K

Keillor, Garrison 14

L

LaHaye, Tim and Jenkins, Jerry 17, 18, 19
Lasch, Christopher 42
Law 64
LeMarquand, Grant 100, 102
Lerner, Rabbi Michael 97
Lucifer 51
Luther, Martin 6–7, 16, 17, 19, 60

M

MacDonald, George 4, 27, 29, 30, 33, 101
Magic (deep) 27f, 31
Marcionism 85
Magnificat 23f, 104
Mandala, Nelson 44, 46
Marxism 54
Medieval worldview 49
Middle East Conflict 18, 70, 79, 99, 104
Midrash 97
Miller, Donald 58
Missional strategy 50, 51, 57
Myth 28

N

Narnia 17, 19, 29, 30, 31, 36, 37, 39,
        43–48, 51, 55, 56, 76, 86
Nazi Germany 67
Newbigin, Lesslie 54
Newell, Marilee 19
Newton, John 44

O

Owen, Wilfred 97

P

Pagan myths 27
Pascal, Blaise 65, 66

Pelagian repentance 35
Pentacostalism 53
Pepys, Samuel 87
Pfister, Oscar 103
Prayer
　　to Abba Father 41, 46, 48, 90,
　　the Lord's prayer 105–16
　　Mary's prayer 20
　　and the church's mission 53, 105
　　for one's opponents 104,

R

Rand, Ayn 43
Reformation 16
Response and Responsibility 14–21
Ringer, Robert 42
Roman Catholicism 93
Rowling, J. K. 22
Ruskin, John 22
Rossetti, Dante Gabriel 13

S

Sacrifice 26
Sayers, George 52
Sayers, Dorothy 21
Schleiermacher, Friedrich 13, 22
Scotland 74
Smails, Thomas 30
Slavery 39–48
South Africa 44

T

Taizé 85
Temple, William 60
Thiselton, Anthony 6
Theodicy 65
Thielicke, Helmut 66, 67, 68, 70
Till We Have Faces, 37, 76, 77, 78
Tolkien, J. R. R. 21, 22, 25, 26, 29, 33, 38,
　　56, 60
Torrance, J. B. 74, 75

U

United States 43, 45, 58, 59, 60, 79

V

Vietnam War 11

W

Wilberforce, William 44, 46
Williams, Charles 3
Williams, Rowan 45, 46
Wordsworth, William 3
World War I 59, 98
World War II 67–70
Wright, N. T. (Tom) 21, 45, 101